Computer Network Security and Cyber Ethics

Computer Network Security and Cyber Ethics

by
JOSEPH MIGGA KIZZA

McFarland & Company, Inc., Publishers
Jefferson, North Carolina, and London

Celebrating what is good within us.
Keep the flame burning!

Library of Congress Cataloguing-in-Publication Data

Kizza, Joseph Migga.
    Computer network security and cyber ethics / by
Joseph Migga Kizza.
        p.   cm.
    Includes bibliographical references and index.
    ISBN 0-7864-1134-1 (softcover : 50# alkaline paper) ∞
    1. Computer networks — Security measures.   2. Internet —
Moral and ethical aspects.   3. Computer crimes.   I. Title.
TK5105.59.K58   2002
005.8 — dc21   2001044621

British Library cataloguing data are available

Manufactured in the United States of America

Cover image ©2001 Art Today

*McFarland & Company, Inc., Publishers
  Box 611, Jefferson, North Carolina 28640
  www.mcfarlandpub.com*

Contents

Acknowledgments

I am very grateful to all colleagues for the ideas, suggestions, and criticism they freely gave to me.

I am indebted to my daughters Josephine and Florence, and to my dear wife, *Omumbejja* Immaculate, for her input and support. She was instrumental in many ways.

Finally, to all those who, in one way or another, contributed towards this project, but whose names do not appear, thanks.

Preface

It's the old joke in security: Nobody gets a radar detector until after they get a ticket. — Frank Prince, analyst, Forrester Research

Our increasing reliance and dependence on computer and telecommunications technology is slowly making cyberspace a critical component of our national security and social well-being. All critical components of the national infrastructure, including telecommunication, electrical power grids, gas and oil storage and transportation, water supply systems, banking and finance, transportation, and emergency services that include medical, police, fire, and rescue, are connected in some way to cyberspace. This connection makes cyberspace an important security concern, not only to those in government and those charged with the security of the nation, but to all of us, for our individual security and well-being. The potential of a kind of "cyber Pearl Harbor" attack is high.

The "distributed denial of service" (DDoS) attacks on Internet heavyweights and popular sites such as Yahoo!, leading retailers Buy.com, eBay and Amazon.com, and the news site CNN.com, and the lightning-like strike of global computers by the Philippine-generated "Love Bug," all show how easy it is to launch an attack and how difficult it is to protect cyberspace resources. The military and indeed the government cannot do it alone. It must be a joint effort of all of us.

Although the DDoS cyber attacks did not involve system penetration into critical components of the national infrastructure, the time it took the law enforcement agencies to apprehend the criminals, together with the ease

1

with which the Manila-generated "Love Bug" and the "Killer Resume" penetrated and crippled global computer networks, and the circus-like atmosphere that surrounded the arrest of the "Love Bug" creator, are indicative of the chaos we are in. These incidents show how unprepared we are for a cyber attack, and are also a good measure of how far we have to go to make cyberspace safe for all.

If the recent trend in cyber attacks is any indication, we are in for an avalanche of cyber vandalism as society becomes more dependent on computer networks. The rate of cyber vandalism, both reported and unreported, is on the rise. Organized attacks, such as those mentioned above and similar ones like "Solar Sunrise" on Defense Department computers in February 1998, and computer viruses such as Melissa and W32/Mypics which preyed on Microsoft software, are increasing. According to the General Accounting Office, the number of security incidents handled by Carnegie Mellon University's CERT Coordination Center, a federally funded emergency response team, is on the rise, growing from 1,334 in 1993 to 4,398 during the first half of 1999.

The rise in such incidents is an indication of the poor state of our cyberspace security policy and the vulnerability of all cyberspace resources. Yet there are no signs on the horizon to indicate a slowdown in the attacks. Indeed all predictions are that they are likely to continue because of the following reasons:

- Cyberspace infrastructure and communication protocols are inherently weak.
- The average user in cyberspace has very limited knowledge of the computer network infrastructure, its weaknesses and gaping loopholes.
- Society, as a whole, is increasingly becoming irreversibly dependent on an infrastructure and technology that it little understands.
- There are no long-term (let alone immediate) plans or mechanisms in place to educate the public.
- There is a high degree of complacency in a society that still accords a "whiz kid" status to cyberspace vandals.
- The only known remedies to attacks consist of patching loopholes after an attack has occurred.
- Reporting is voluntary and haphazard.
- The nation has yet to understand the seriousness of cyber vandalism and what the cost may be.

If we as a society are concerned about individual as well as collective security, privacy and civil liberties, we need to start finding solutions. A good national cyberspace security policy is needed to:

(i)   make everyone aware of their vulnerability and the consequences of a cyberspace attack to their well-being;

(ii) ensure that everyone is well equipped to deal with a cyber attack and to live safely in this technology-driven and fast-changing society;

(iii) help put in place a set of mechanisms to detect, prevent, and handle any cyber attack; and

(iv) devise a legal and regulatory framework to handle cyberspace's social consequences.

This book will focus on these four security issues with the intent of increasing the public's awareness of the magnitude of cyber vandalism, the weaknesses and loopholes inherent in the cyberspace infrastructure, and the ways to protect ourselves and our society. The goal is public understanding of the nature and motives of cyber acts, how such acts are committed, and the efforts being undertaken to prevent future occurrences. These issues are covered in six chapters.

Chapter 1, "Cyberspace Infrastructure," attempts to demystify the infra-structure that forms the backbone of a computer communication network like the Internet, the underlying communication protocols, and the jargon of application software that runs on these networks. The chapter walks the reader through cyberspace, enabling him or her to exit the premises with a firm knowledge of the topology and an understanding of the underlying weak-nesses and loopholes in structure and protocol.

Chapter 2, "Anatomy of the Problem," focuses on the root causes, with emphasis on the public's lack of knowledge of cyberspace infrastructure and communication protocols, society's increasing dependence on computers and computer related technologies, the lack of a sound mechanism to educate the masses, the "whiz kid" status bestowed on cyber vandals, and other issues.

Chapter 3, "Types of Cyber Attacks," discusses cyber attacks in gen-eral based on past attacks which are categorized according to their nature, the motives involved, and the architecture including one-to-one, many-to-one, one-to-many and many-to-many.

Chapter 4, "Cyber Crimes: Costs and Social Consequences," broadens the discussion of the previous chapter to estimate costs involved. The costs include financial, psychological, moral and material losses. The chapter also discuses the consequences of cyber attacks on individuals, businesses, and the nation.

Chapter 5, "Cyber Crimes: Prevention, Detection, and System Surviva-bility," continues the discussion of cyber crimes with an extended discussion and corresponding analysis of the current legislative, educational, self-regula-tion and enforcement efforts at local, state, national, and multinational levels.

Chapter 6, "Cyberspace and Cyber Ethics Today and Beyond," sums up our discussion of cyber crimes by looking at the state of cyberspace, ethics in cyberspace, the current technological challenges to our social infrastructures, the planned overhaul of the Internet, and the social consequences of such new technology. A number of ethical and social issues are raised, inviting the reader to reflect on the direction of technology and the associated legal, economic, and social implications.

In summary the book attempts to:

(i)   alert the public to the magnitude of cyberspace vandalism and the weaknesses and loopholes inherent in the cyberspace infrastructure;

(ii) evaluate the effectiveness of the current cyberspace security policies as they affect society, and discuss the planned "new" cyberspace and its consequences; and

(iii) start a debate on what the future cyberspace should be and how it should safeguard our security and well-being.

The book is intended to be a teaching and reference tool for anyone interested in cyberspace social and ethical issues and the available techniques to deal with cyber crimes. An appendix of "Exercise Questions for Classroom Use" is offered for teachers wishing to work with the book in an institutional setting. Because the book gives a detailed account of the state of cyberspace today, it should serve as a good reference and source of ideas for computer network security personnel and policy makers. The book will give the reader a good understanding of the state of cyber security, or in some cases the lack thereof, leaving room for active readers to suggest additional measures needed to secure cyberspace. Valid cyberspace security issues are raised, including possible violation of individual rights, the limited scope and the inadequacy of current cyberspace security techniques, and the lack of a serious campaign to educate the public.

The book targets college students in computer science, information science, technology studies, library sciences, and engineering, as well as students in other areas who are interested in information technology. Professionals, especially those working in information-intensive areas, will likewise find the book a good reference source. It will also be valuable to those interested in any aspect of cyberspace security and those simply wanting to become cyberspace literate.

Joseph Migga Kizza
Chattanooga, Tennessee
September 2001

Chapter 1

Cyberspace Infrastructure

In his science fiction novel *Neuromancer,* William Gibson first coined the term "cyberspace" to describe his vision of a three-dimensional space of pure information, moving between computer and computer clusters that make up this vast landscape. This infrastructure, as envisioned by Gibson, links computers as both computing and transmitting elements, people as generators and users of information, and pure information moving at high speed between highly independent transmitting elements. Before we go into a full discussion of how pure information is really generated and how it moves in cyberspace, let us take a look at a simple but highly instructive scenario that works by using similar structures and principles like those used in cyberspace.

An Introductory Scenario

Suppose you want to communicate with your Aunt Kay who lives a few thousand miles from you. You have an array of choices to do this but let us assume that you decide on writing and posting your message through the good old snail mail. Writing involves a number of operational procedures, the major ones being the following:

- You write a letter and put it in an envelope, on which you write your aunt's destination address and your return address.

- You or somebody takes the letter to either a mailbox or a post office.
- The post mail carrier accesses the mailbox and takes your letter to a sorting center.
- Mail will be sorted and grouped.
- The group with your letter may be tracked to an airport or tracked all the way to the destination post office.
- If tracked to the airport, it will be deposited at the airport.
- An aircraft will carry it to a destination airport and eventually to the destination post office.
- Postal carriers at the destination post office will retrieve your letter, together with others.
- It will be sorted to identify the route according to your aunt's street address or box number.
- The route carrier will take the letter to your aunt's mailbox.
- Your aunt or somebody else will retrieve the letter from the mailbox.
- Your aunt will open and read the letter.

Figure 1.1 shows a graphical representation of the mail operational procedures of the postal system described.

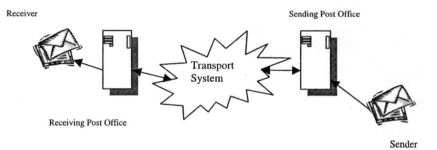

Figure 1.1 Graphical Representation of Mail Operational Procedures

Every one of the mail operational procedures we have listed is usually done in exactly the same way, whatever the source or destination of the letter. The messages, as they travel from source to destination, go through a number of stations, and at each station specific procedures are performed. These operational procedures we will call protocols. As messages move through the postal system, underlying protocols performed at one station must rely on protocols performed on the previous station. For example the protocols performed at the mailbox by the mail carrier to take the message from the mailbox to the sorting center are based on the assumption that the protocols at the previous station, those of moving the message from the writer to the mailbox, were performed. And the protocols to move the message to the mailbox depend on the performance of protocols at the station before it, those of writing and packaging that message.

The number of stations a message goes through from source to destination can be clearly portioned into two sets, one set on the receiving side and the other at the sending end. The activities performed at each station determine the positioning of the station in the set. If we follow this model, two interesting observations can be made: one, that the order of stations in each set make up a stack, and two, that one stack is a mirror image of the other stack. Figure 1.2 shows the dual stacked activities of the postal system.

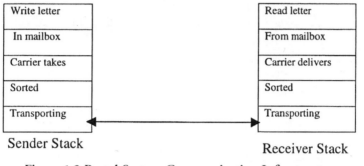

Figure 1.2 Postal System Communication Infrastructure

From Figure 1.2 we make the following observations:

- That from every protocol at the sending host, there is a corresponding protocol at the receiving host.
- That the protocols at the same level on both ends are the same.
- That each protocol station in the stack uses the protocols in the upper stations.
- If a protocol in one station is not performed, all other protocols that follow that station are not carried out which renders the delivery from this point on unworkable.
- Weaknesses and failures in each layer and indeed each station in the delivery system result in corresponding weaknesses and failures in the next set of protocols in the stack and eventually in the corresponding protocol stack of the receiving end.
- Bad protocols lead to inoperable or bad forwarding delivery systems.

Our scenario displays three identifiable components:

- The infrastructure made up of the basic physical entities like mailboxes, mail carriers, roads, trucks, planes, airports, sorting machines, and airport sky routes.
- Operational procedures to include:
  - (i) application — consisting of message creation, packaging, unpacking, and reading.
  - (ii) posting — consisting of physical movement of the messages to and from mailboxes.
  - (iii) sorting — involving the movement of messages from mailboxes to the sorting centers.
  - (iv) transport — consisting of moving the messages via trucks, in planes, and other methods.
  - (v) linkage — consisting of connecting links like roads, air routes and others.
- A pair of protocols stacks — stacks of operational procedures at both the sending and receiving end hosts. The protocols in each station in the stack are different but each protocol is based on the protocols of the previous station. For example the protocols the mail-carrier follows to collect your mail from your mailbox are based on the assumption that somebody really put the message in the mailbox. These protocols, in turn, depend on the protocols from the previous station that somebody really wrote a letter to be sent to the mailbox. This way then the postal system protocols are always in stacks and they are always followed in order at each end of the communication line.

In this scenario, we have left out many more details. For example we do not know whether the letter was certified or registered, requiring that a confirmation or an acknowledgment be sent back to the sender. We left out a lot of low level activities taking place between the source post office and the destination post office. The major activities outlined above and all the underlying mundane details are essentially unknown to both the sender and the recipient of the letter. It is better that way and the post system was designed to work that way so that it does not make users worried with the unnecessary details.

Lack of knowledge about the postal system does not seem to worry many users very much. In fact I would not like to bother myself every time I post a letter with the details of how my letter is moved from my mailbox en route to its destination. Details like whether the mail carrier comes in a car or on a bike, or whether my letter is taken by a truck or by a plane, are not important to me as long as my letter arrives in one piece, in time, at its intended address. A number of reasons may account for this complacence:

- The postal system is government owned, and people like to believe in their governments to the point of making them infallible. To such people, the postal system is safe as long it is run by their government.
- The postal system, for a long time, has been the only kid on the block. They have grown up with it, and as far as they know it has been delivering in snow, rain, and hailstorm.
- There have been, as far as we know, no pre-teens and teens trying to break into any post office for fun or to challenge the security of the postal facilities.
- It is common knowledge that there is hardly anything of value in postal facilities besides piles of mail and stamps.
- On a large scale, technological developments that swept through the workplace seem to have avoided the postal system, so there are no major technological temptations and challenges to its activities.
- If anybody ever attempts to break into a postal facility, whether caught or not, people will call such a person a contemptible fool, not an admirable "whiz" by any measure.

For these and other reasons, the postal system is believed to be safe and probably efficient, and it seems to deliver. So why worry whether you understand its infrastructure or not? Unfortunately this is not the case with the computer communication system we want to focus on in this chapter.

The postal system infrastructure and protocols, though not exactly the same, have many striking similarities with the computer communication network infrastructure as we will see in later discussions. It is because of these close similarities that the scenario above was chosen to lead us into the computer communication network system.

Computer Communication Networks

A computer communication network system consists of hardware, software, and humanware. The hardware and software allow the humanware — the users — to create, exchange, and use information. The hardware consists of a collection of nodes that include the end systems, commonly called hosts, intermediate switching elements that include hubs, bridges, routers and gateways, and we will collectively call all these network or computing elements, or sometimes without loss of generality, just network elements. The software, all application programs and network protocols, synchronize and coordinate the sharing and exchange of data among the network elements and the sharing of expensive resources in the network. Network elements, network software, and users, all work together so that individual users get to exchange messages and share resources on other systems that are not readily available locally. The network elements may be of diverse hardware technologies and the software may be as different as possible, but the whole combo must work together in unison. This concept that allows multiple, diverse underlying hardware technologies, and different software regimes to interconnect heterogeneous networks and bring them to communicate is called *internetworking* technology. Internetworking technology makes Gibson's vision a reality; it makes possible the movement and exchange of data and the sharing of resources among the network elements. This is achieved through the low-level mechanisms provided by the network elements and high-level communication facilities provided by the software running on the communicating elements. Let us see how this infrastructure works by looking at the hardware and software components and how they produce a working computer communication network. We will start with the hardware components, consisting of network types, and network topology. Later we will discuss the software components consisting of the transmission control system.

Network Types

The connected computer network elements may be each independently connected on the network, or connected in small clusters which are in turn connected together to form bigger networks via connecting devices. The size of the cluster determines the network type. There are, in general, two network types; the local area network (LAN) and a wide area network (WAN). A LAN consists of network elements in a small geographical area such as a building floor, a building, or a few adjacent buildings. The advantage of a LAN is that all network elements are close together so the communication links maintain a higher speed data movement. Also because of the proximity of the communicating elements, high cost and quality communicating elements can be used to deliver better service and high reliability. Figure 1.3 shows a LAN network.

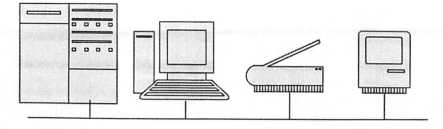

Figure 1.3 A LAN

WANs cover large geographical areas. Some advantages of a WAN include distributing services to a wider community and availability of a wide array of both hardware and software resources that may not be available in a LAN. However, because of the large geographical areas covered by WANs, communication media are slow and often unreliable. Figure 1.4 shows a WAN network.

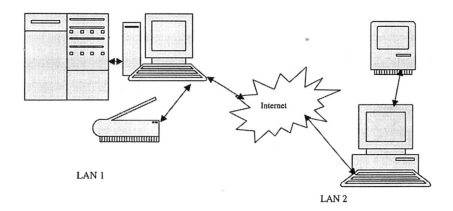

Figure 1.4 A WAN Network

Network Topology

WAN networks are typically found in two topologies: mesh and tree. WANs using a mesh topology provide multiple access links between network elements. The multiplicity of access links offers an advantage in network reliability because whenever a network element failure occurs, the network can always find a by-pass to the failed element and the network continues to function. Figure 1.5 shows a mesh network.

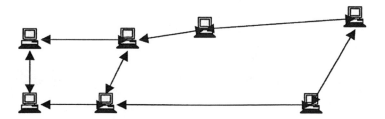

Figure 1.5 Mesh Network

A WAN using a tree topology uses a hierarchical structure in which the most predominant element is the root of the tree and all other elements in the network share a child-parent relationship. The tree topology is a generalization of the bus topology. As in ordinary trees, there are no closed loops, so dealing with failures can be tricky especially in deeply rooted trees. Transmission from any element in the network propagates through the network and is received by all elements in the network. Figure 1.6 shows WAN using a tree topology.

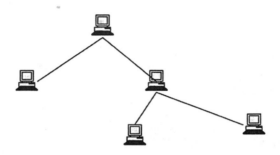

Figure 1.6 Tree Topology

A LAN can be a bus, a star, or ring topology. Elements in a bus topology, as seen below in Figure 1.7, are on a shared bus and, therefore, have equal access to all LAN resources. All network elements have full-duplex connections to the transmitting medium which allow them to send and receive data. Because each computing element is directly attached to the transmitting medium, a transmission from any one element propagates the whole length of the medium in either direction and, therefore, can be received by all elements in the network. Because of this, precautions need to be taken to make sure that transmissions intended for one element can only be gotten by that element and no one else. Also if two or more elements try to transmit at the same time, there is a mechanism to deal with the likely collision

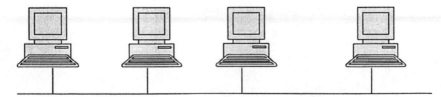

Figure 1.7 Bus Topology

of signals and to bring a quick recovery from such a collision. It is also necessary to create fairness in the network so that all other elements can transmit when they need to do so.

To improve efficiency in LANs that use a bus topology, only one element in the network can have control of the bus at any one time. This requirement prevents collision from occurring in the network as elements in the network try to seize the bus at the same time.

In a star topology setting, all elements in the network are connected to a central element. However, elements are interconnected as pairs in a point-to-point manner through this central element, and communication between any pair of elements must go through this central element. The central element or node can operate either in a broadcast fashion in which case information from one element is broadcast to all connected elements or it can transmit as a switching device in which the incoming data are transmitted to only one element, the nearest element en route to the destination. The biggest disadvantage to the star topology in networks is that the failure of the central element results in the failure of the entire network. Figure 1.8 shows a star topology.

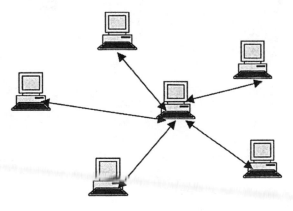

Figure 1.8 Star Topology

In networks using a ring topology, each computing element is directly connected to the transmitting medium via a uni-directional connection so that information put on the transmission medium is able to reach all computing elements in the network through a system of taking turns in sending information around the ring. Figure 1.9 shows a ring topology network. The taking of turns in passing information is managed through a token system. An element currently sending information has control of the token and

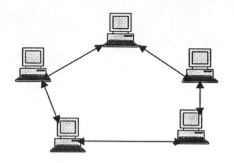

Figure 1.9 Ring Topology Network

it passes it downstream to its nearest neighbor after its turn. The token system is a good management system of collision and fairness.

There are variations of a ring topology collectively called *hub* hybrids. They can be a combination of either a star with a bus as shown in Figure 1.10 (a) or a stretched star as shown in Figure 1.10 (b).

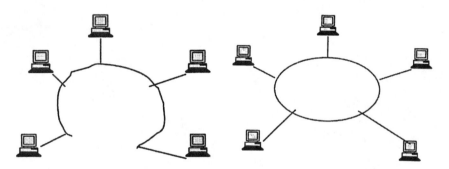

Figure 1.10 (a), left, Hub Consisting of a Bus and Star Topologies.
Figure 1.10 (b), right, Token Ring Hub

Although network topologies are important in LANs, the choice of a topology depends on a number of other factors including the type of transmission medium, reliability of the network, and the size of the network and its anticipated future growth. Recently the most popular LAN topologies have been the bus, star, and ring topologies. The most popular bus and star-based LAN topology is the Ethernet and the most popular ring-based LAN topology is the Token Ring.

Ethernet as a LAN technology started in the mid–1970s. Since then, it has grown at a rapid rate to capture a far larger LAN technology market share than its rivals which include Asynchronous Transfer Mode (ATM), Fiber

Distributed Data Interface (FDDI), and Token Ring technologies. Its rapid growth is partly historical in that it has been on the market for the longest period and it is simple. Many variations of Ethernet use either a bus or a star topology and can run over any of the following transmission media: coaxial cable, twisted pair, and optical fiber. We will discuss transmission media in the coming sections.

Ethernet can transmit data at different speeds varying from a few Mbps to 1Gbps. The basic Ethernet transmission structure is a frame and it is shown in Figure 1.11 below.

Other control headers	Destination address	Source address	Type	Data	Error detection (CRC)

Figure 1.11 Ethernet Frame Data Structure

The source and destination fields contain 6 bytes LAN addresses of the form xx-xx-xx-xx-xx-xx, where x is a hexadecimal integer. The error detection field is four bytes of bits used for error detection, usually using Cyclic Redundancy Check (CRC) algorithm, in which the source and destination elements synchronize the values of these bits. We will discuss CRC in Chapter 5.

Ethernet LANs broadcast data to all network elements. Because of this, Ethernet uses a collision and fairness control protocol commonly known as Carrier Sense Multiple Access (CSMA) and Collision Detection (CD), combined as CSMA/CD. CSMA/CD makes sure that an element never transmits a data frame when it senses that some other element on the network is transmitting. In this case it is carrier sensitive. If an element detects another element on the network transmitting, the detecting element immediately aborts its efforts. It then tries to retransmit later after a random amount of time. Table 1.1 below shows some of popular Ethernet technologies.

Technology	Transmission medium	Topology	Speed
10 Base2	Coaxial	Bus	10Mbps
10 BaseT	Twisted	Star	10Mbps
100 BaseT	Copperwire	Star	100Mbps
Gigabit	Optical fiber	Star	Gigabps

Table 1.1 Popular Ethernet Technologies

Token Ring LAN technology is based on a token concept which involves passing the token around the network so that all network elements have equal access to it. The token concept is very similar to a worshipping house collection basket. If and when an attendee wants to donate money during the service, they wait until the basket makes its way to where they are sitting. At that point the donor grabs the basket and puts in money. Precisely, when the network element wants to transmit, it waits for the token on the ring to make its way to the element's connection point on the ring. When the token arrives at this point, the element grabs it and changes one bit of the token which becomes the start bit in the data frame the element will be transmitting. The element then inserts data and releases the payload onto the ring. It then waits for the token to make a round and come back. Upon return, the element withdraws the token and a new token is put on the ring for another network element that may need to transmit.

Because of its round-robin nature, the token ring technique gives each network element a fair chance of transmitting if it wants to. However, if the token ever gets lost, the network business gets halted. Figure 1.12 shows the structure of a token data frame.

Start field	Access control	Source address	Destination address	Data	Ending field

Figure 1.12 Token Data Frame

Technology	Transmission medium	Topology	Speed
1	Twisted pair	Ring	4Mbps
2	Twisted	Ring	16Mbps
3	Twisted pair	Ring	100Mbps
4	Optical fiber	Ring	100Mbps

Table 1.2 Token Ring Technologies

Like Ethernet, Token Ring has a variety of technologies based on transmission rates. Table 1.2 above shows some of these topologies [1].

Beside Ethernet and Token Ring technologies, there are other LAN technologies. One is Fiber Distributed Data Interface (FDDI), which uses a token ring scheme with many similarities to the original token ring technology. Another is Asynchronous Transfer Mode (ATM), with the goal to transport real time voice and video, text, e-mail, and graphic data. ATM offers a full array of network services that make it a rival of the Internet network.

Transmission Control Systems (TCS)

The performance of a network type depends greatly on the transmission control system the network uses. Network transmission control systems have five components: transmission technology, transmission media, connecting devices, communication services, and transmission protocols.

Transmission Technology

Data movement in a computer network is either analog or digital. In an analog format, data is sent as continuous electromagnetic waves on an interval representing things like voice and video. In a digital format, data is sent as a digital signal, a sequence of voltage pulses which can be represented as a stream of binary bits. Transmission itself is the propagation and processing of data signals between network elements. The concept of representation of data for transmission, either as analog or digital signal, is called an encoding scheme. Encoded data is then transmitted over a suitable transmission medium that connects all network elements. There are two encoding schemes, analog and digital. Analog encoding propagates analog signals representing analog data. Digital encoding on the other hand propagates digital signals representing either an analog or a digital signal representing digital data of binary streams. Because our interest in this book is in digital networks, we will focus on the encoding of digital data.

In an analog encoding of digital data, the encoding scheme uses a continuous oscillating wave, usually a sine wave, with a constant frequency signal called a carrier signal. Carrier signals have three characteristics: amplitude, frequency, and phase shift. The scheme then uses a modem, a modulation-demodulation pair to modulate and demodulate any one of the three carrier characteristics. Figure 1.13 shows the three carrier characteristic modulations [1].

- Amplitude modulation represents each binary value by a different amplitude of the carrier frequency. For example, as Figure 1.13 (a) shows, the absence of or low carrier frequency may represent a 0 and any other frequency then represents a 1.
- Frequency modulation also represents the two binary values by two different frequencies close to the frequency of the underlying carrier. Higher frequency represent a 1 and low frequency then represent a 0. Frequency modulation is represented in Figure 1.13 (b) below.
- Phase shift modulation changes the timing of the carrier wave, shifting the carrier phase to encode the data. One type of shifting may

represent a 0 and another type a 1. For example, as Figure 1.13 (c) shows, a 0 may represent a forward shift and a 1 may represent a backward shift.

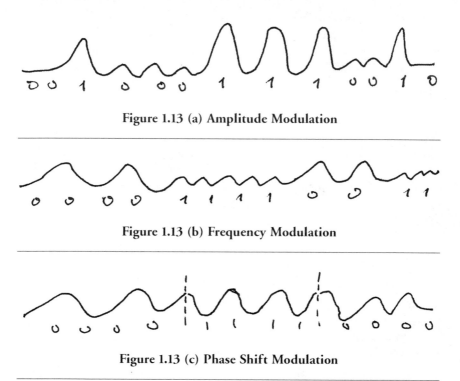

Figure 1.13 (a) Amplitude Modulation

Figure 1.13 (b) Frequency Modulation

Figure 1.13 (c) Phase Shift Modulation

Quite often during transmission of data over a network medium, it may happen that the volume of transmitted data far exceeds the capacity of the medium. When this happens, it may be possible to make multiple signal carriers share a transmission medium. This is referred to as *multiplexing.* There are two ways multiplexing can be achieved: time-division multiplexing (TDM) and frequency-division multiplexing (FDM).

The second encoding scheme is the *digital encoding of digital data.* Before information is transmitted, it is converted into bits(zeros and ones). The bits are then sent to a receiver as electrical or optical signals. The scheme uses two different voltages to represent the two binary states (digits). For example a negative voltage may be used to represent a 1 and a positive voltage to represent a 0. Figure 1.14 shows the encoding of digital data using this scheme.

digital data using this scheme.

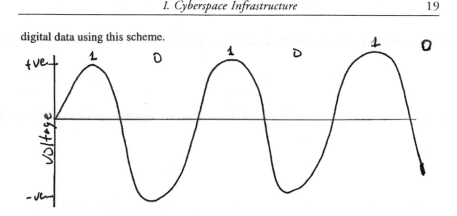

Figure 1.14 Encoding Electrical Signals and Showing of Zeros and Ones

To insure a uniform standard for using electrical signals to represent data, a standard was developed by Electrical Industries Association (EIA) and it is widely known as *RS–232*. RS–232 is a serial, asynchronous communication standard; serial because during transmission, bits follow one another, and asynchronous because it is irregular in the rate of transfer of data bits. The bits are put in a form of a packet and the packets are transmitted. RS–232 works in full-duplex between the two transmitting elements. This means that the two elements can both send and receive data simultaneously. RS–232 has a number of limitations including the idealizing of voltages, which never exists, and limits on both bandwidth and distances.

Transmission Media

The transmission medium is the physical medium between network elements. The characteristic quality, dependability, and overall performance of a network depends heavily on its transmission medium. Transmission medium determines a network's key criteria, the distance covered, and the transmission rate. Computer network transmission media fall into two categories: wired and wireless transmission [2].

Wired transmission consists of different types of physical media. A very common medium, for example, is *optical fiber*, a small medium made up of glass and plastics and it conducts an optical ray. As shown in Figure 1.15 (a), a simple optical fiber has a central core made up of thin fibers of glass or plastics. The fibers are protected by a glass or plastic coating called a *cladding*. The cladding, though made up of the same materials as the core, has different properties that give it the capacity to reflect back to the core rays that tangentially hit on it. The cladding itself is encased in a plastic jacket. The jacket is meant to protect the inner fiber from external abuses like bending and abrasions.

The transmitted light is emitted at the source either from a light emitting diode (LED) or an injection laser diode (ILD). At the receiving end, the emitted rays are received by a photo detector.

Another physical medium is the *twisted pair*, two insulated copper wires wrapped around each other forming frequent and numerous twists. Together, the twisted, insulated copper wires act as a full-duplex communication link. To increase the capacity of the transmitting medium, more than one pair of the twisted wires may be bundled together in a protective coating. Twisted pairs are far less expensive than optical fibers, and indeed other media and they are, therefore, widely used in telephone and computer networks. However, they are limited in transmission rate, distance, and bandwidth. Figure 1.15 (c) shows a twisted pair.

Coaxial cables are dual conductor cables with an inner conductor in the core of the cable protected by an insulation layer and the outer conductor surrounding the insulation. The outer conductor is itself protected by yet another outer coating called the sheath. Figure 1.15 (a) shows a coaxial cable. Coaxial cables are commonly used in television transmissions. Unlike twisted pairs, coaxial cables can be used over long distances.

A traditional medium for wired communication is *copper wires*, which have been used in communication because of their low resistance to electrical currents which allow signals to travel even further. But copper wires suffer from interference from electromagnetic energy from the environment, including from themselves. Because of this, copper wires are insulated.

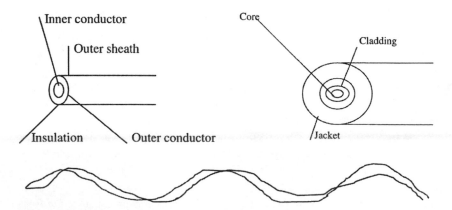

Figure 1.15 (a), above left, Coaxial Cable. Figure 1.15 (b), above right, Optical Fiber. Figure 1.15(c), directly above, Twisted Pair.

Wireless communication involves basic media like radio wave communication, satellite communication, laser beam, microwave, and infrared [3]. Radio, of course, is familiar to us all as radio broadcasting. Networks using radio communications use electromagnetic radio waves or radio frequency commonly referred to as RF transmissions. RF transmissions are very good for long distances when combined with satellites to refract the radio waves.

Microwave, infrared, and laser are other communication types that can be used in computer networks. Microwaves are a higher frequency version of radio waves but whose transmissions, unlike the radio, can be focused in a single direction. Infrared is best used effectively in a small confined area, for example in a room as you communicate with your television remote which uses infrared signals. Laser light transmissions can be used to carry data through air and optical fibers but like microwaves they must be refracted when used over large distances.

Cell-based communication technology of cellular telephones and personal communication services like palms are boosting this wireless communication. Wireless communication is also being boosted by the development in broadband multimedia services that use satellite communication.

Network Connecting Devices

Computing elements in either LAN or WAN clusters are brought together by and can communicate through connecting devices commonly referred to as network *nodes*. Nodes in a network are either at the ends as end systems commonly known as clients, or in the middle of the network as transmitting elements. Among the most common connecting devises are: hubs, bridges, switches, routers, and gateways. Let us briefly look at each one of these devices.

A hub is the simplest in the family of network connecting devices because it connects LAN components with identical protocols. It takes in imports and re-transmits them verbatim. It can be used to switch both digital and analog data. In each node, pre-setting must be done to prepare for the formatting of the incoming data. For example if the incoming data is in digital format, the hub must pass it on as packets; however, if the incoming data is analog, then the hub passes it in a signal form. There are two types of hubs: simple and multiple port hubs. Figure 1.16 shows the types and positions of hubs in a LAN.

Bridges are like hubs in every respect including the fact that they connect LAN components with identical protocols. However, bridges filter incoming data packets for addresses before they are forwarded, now as data *frames*. As it filters the data packets, the bridge makes no modifications to

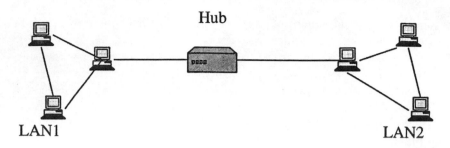

Figure 1.16 (a) A Simple Hub

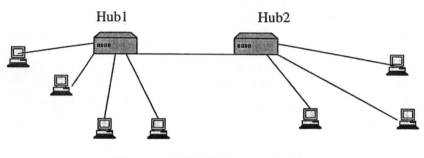

Figure 1.16 (b) Multi-Ported Hubs

the format and content of the incoming data. A bridge filters frames to determine whether a frame should be forwarded or dropped. It works like a postal sorting machine which checks the mail for correct full postal addresses and drops mail if either no forwarding address or the address is illegible. The bridge filters and forwards frames on the network with the help of a dynamic bridge table. The bridge table, which is initially empty, maintains the LAN addresses for each computer in the LAN and the addresses of each bridge interface that connects the LAN to other LANs. Bridges, like hubs, can be either simple or multi-ported. Figure 1.17 shows the position of a bridge in a network cluster. Figure 1.17 (a) shows a simple bridge while Figure 1.17 (b) multi-ported bridge.

LAN addresses on each frame in the bridge table are of the form cc-cc-cc-cc-cc-cc-cc-cc, where cc are hexadecimal integers. Each LAN address in the cluster uniquely connects a computer on a bridge. LAN addresses for each machine in a cluster are actually network identification card (NIC) numbers which are unique for any network card ever manufactured. The bridge table, which initially is empty, has a turnaround time slice of n seconds, and node addresses and their corresponding interfaces enter and leave

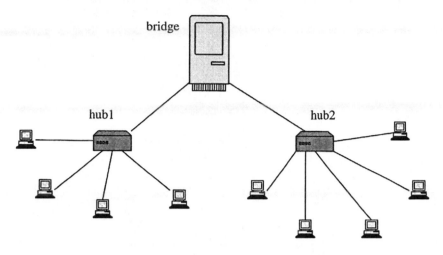

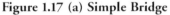

Figure 1.17 (a) Simple Bridge

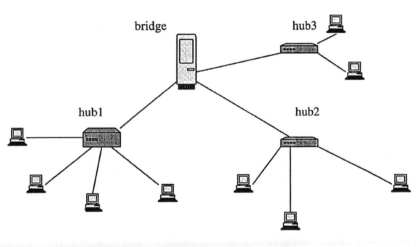

Figure 1.17 (b) Multi-Ported Bridge

the table after n seconds [4]. For example suppose in Figure 1.18 we begin with an empty bridge table and node A in cluster 1 with the address A0-15-7A-ES-15-00 sending a frame to the bridge via interface 1 at time 00:50. This address becomes the first entry in the bridge table, Table 1.3, and it will be purged from the table after n seconds. The bridge uses these node addresses in the table to filter and then forwards LAN frames onto the rest of the network.

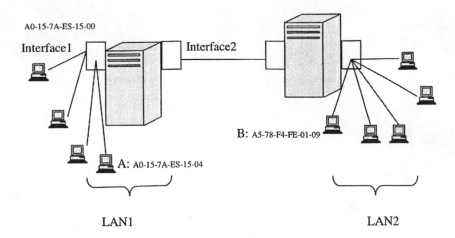

Figure 1.18 LAN with Two Interfaces

Address	Interface	Time
A0-15-7A-ES-15-00	1	00:50

Table 1.3 Changes in the Bridge Table

Switches are newer network intercommunication devices that are nothing more than high-performance bridges. Besides high performance, switches accommodate a high number of interfaces. They can, therefore, interconnect a relatively high number of hosts and clusters. Like their cousins, the bridges, switches filter and then forward frames.

Routers are general purpose devices that interconnect two or more heterogeneous networks. They are usually dedicated to special purposes computers with separate input and output interfaces for each connected network. Each network addresses the router as a member computer in that network. Because routers and gateways are the backbone of large computer networks like the Internet, they have special features that give them the flexibility and the ability to cope with varying network addressing schemes and frame sizes through segmentation of big packets into smaller sizes that fit the new network components. They can also cope with both software and hardware interfaces and are very reliable. Since each router can connect two or more heterogeneous networks, each router is a member of each network it connects to. It, therefore, has a network host address for that network and an interface address for each network it is connected to. Because of this rather strange characteristic, each router interface has its own Address Resolution Protocol (ARP) module, its LAN address (Network Card Address), and its own Internet Protocol (IP) address.

The router, with the use of a router table, has some knowledge of possible routes a packet could take from its source to its destination. The routing table, like in the bridge and switch, grows dynamically as activities in the network develop. Upon receipt of a packet, the router removes the packet headers and trailers and analyzes the IP header by determining the source and destination addresses, data type, and noting the arrival time. It also updates the router table with new addresses if not already in the table. The IP header and arrival time information is entered in the routing table. Let us explain the working of a router by an example using Figure 1.19.

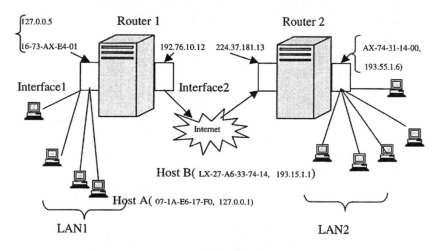

Figure 1.19 Working of a Router

In Figure 1.19, suppose host A tries to send a packet to host B. Host A is in network 1 and host B is in network 2. Both host A and host B have two addresses, the LAN (host) address and IP address. Notice also that the router has two network interfaces: interface 1 for LAN1 and interface 2 for LAN2 for the connection to a bigger network like the Internet. Each interface has a LAN(host) address for the network the interface connects on and a corresponding IP address. As we will see later in the chapter, host A sends a packet to router 1 at time 10:01 that includes, among other things, both its addresses, message type, and destination IP address of host B. The packet is received at interface 1 of the router; the router reads the packet and builds row 1 of the routing table as shown in Table 1.4.

Address	Interface	Time
127.0.0.5	1	10:01
192.76.10.12	2	10:03

Table 1.4 Routing Table

The router notices that the packet is to go to network 193.55.1.***, where *** are digits 0–9, and it has knowledge that this network is connected on interface 2. It forwards the packet to interface 2. Now interface 2 with its own ARP may know host B. If it does, then it forwards the packet on and updates the routing table with inclusion of row 2. What happens when the ARP at the router interface 1 cannot determine the next network? That is, it has no knowledge of the presence of network 193.55.1.***, then it will ask for help from a gateway.

Gateways are more versatile devices that can provide translation between networking technologies such as OSI and TCP/IP (we will discuss these technologies shortly). Because of this, gateways connect two or more autonomous networks each with its own routing algorithms, protocols, domain name service, and network administration procedures and policies. Gateways perform all of the functions of a router and more. In fact a router with added translation functionality is a gateway. The function that does the translation between different network technologies is called a *protocol converter*. Figure 1.20 shows the position of a gateway in a network.

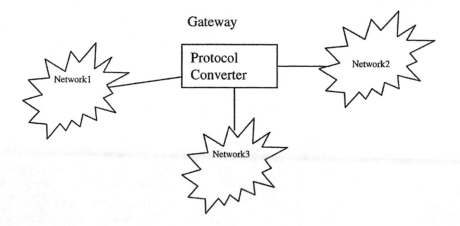

Figure 1.20 Position of a Gateway

Communication Services

Now that we have a network infrastructure in place, how do we get the network transmitting elements to exchange data over the network? The communication control system provides services to meet specific network reliability and efficiency requirements. Two services are provided by most digital networks: connection-oriented and connectionless services.

With a connection-oriented service, before a client can send packets with real data to the server, there must be a three-way handshake. We will discuss the three-way handshake in detail in Chapter 2. For our purpose now, let us just give the general outline. The three-way handshake includes a client initiating the communication by sending the first control packet, the SYN (short for synchronization), with a "hello" to the server's welcoming port. The server creates (opens) a communication socket for further communication with a client and sends a "hello, I am ready" SYN-ACK (short for synchronization-acknowledgment) control packet to the client. Upon receipt of this packet the client then starts to communicate with the server by sending the ACK(short for acknowledgment) control packet usually piggybacked on other data packets. From this point on, either the client or the server can send an onslaught of packets. The connection just established, however, is very loose, and we call this type of connection, not a full connection service, but connection-oriented. Figure 1.21 shows a connection-oriented three-way handshake process.

In a connectionless service there is no handshaking. This means that a client can start to communicate with a server, without warning or inquiry for readiness; it simply sends streams of packets from its sending port to the

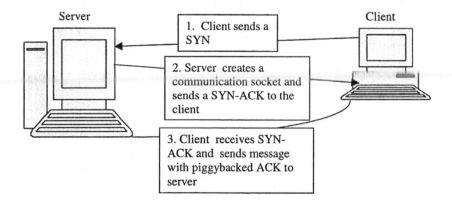

Figure 1.21 Connection-Oriented 3-Way Handshake Process

server's connection port. There are advantages and of course disadvantages to this type of connection service as we discussed in the next section. Briefly, the connection is faster because there is no handshaking which sometimes can be time consuming. However, this service offers no safeguards and guarantees to the sender because there is no prior control information and no acknowledgment.

Before we discuss communication protocols, let us take a detour and briefly discuss data transfer by a switching element. This is a technique by which data is moved from host to host across the length and width of the network mesh of hosts, hubs, bridges, routers, and gateways. This technique is referred to as *data switching*. The type of data switching technique a network uses determines how messages are transmitted between the two communicating elements and across that network. There are two types of data switching techniques: circuit switching and packet switching.

Circuit switching networks reserve the resources needed for the communication session before the session begins. The network establishes a circuit by reserving a constant transmission rate for the duration of transmission. For example, in a telephone communication network a connected line is reserved between the two points before the users can start using the service. One issue of debate on circuit switching is the perceived waste of resources during the so-called silent periods when the connection is fully in force but not being used by the parties. This situation happens when, for example, during a telephone network session, a telephone receiver is not hung up after use, leaving the connection still established. During this period while no one is utilizing the session, the session line is still open.

Packet switching networks on the other hand do not require any resources to be reserved before a communication session begins. Packet switching networks, however, require the sending host to send the message as a packet. If a message is large, it is broken into smaller packets. Then each of the packets is sent on the communication links and across packet switches (routers). Each router, between the sender and receiver, passes the packet on until it reaches the destination server. The destination server reassembles the packets into the final message. Figure 1.22 shows the role of routers in packet switching networks.

Packet switches are considered to be store-and-forward transmitters, meaning they must receive the entire packet before the packet is retransmitted to the next switch. Before we proceed let us make three observations.

- The rate of transmission of a packet between two switching elements depends on the maximum rate of transmission of the link joining them and on the switches themselves.

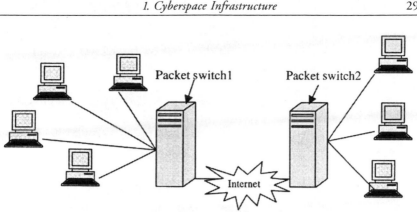

Figure 1.22 Packet Switching Networks

- There are always momentary delays introduced whenever the switch is waiting for a full packet. The longer the packet, the longer the delay.
- Each switching element has a finite buffer for the packets. So it is possible for a packet to arrive only to find the buffer full with other packets. Whenever this happens, the newly arrived packet is not stored but gets lost, a process called *packet drop*. So in peak times, servers may drop a lot of packets. Congestion control techniques use the rate of packet drop as one of the measures of traffic congestion in a network.

Transmission protocols

Packet switching networks are commonly referred to as packet networks for obvious reasons. These networks are also called *asynchronous* networks and in such networks packets are ideal because there is a sharing of the bandwidth, and of course there is no hassle of making reservations for any anticipated transmission. There are two types of packet switching networks. One is the virtual circuit network, in which a packet route is planned and becomes a logical connection before a packet is released. The other is the datagram network, which is the focus of this book.

Because the packet network is very similar to the postal system we discussed early in this chapter, let us draw parallels between the protocols of the postal communication system and those of the packet network or computer network communication system. You may recall that in the postal system, messages were also moved in packets, like envelopes, cards, and boxes. The protocols in the process of moving the letter from your hands to your aunt's hands were put in a stack. In fact we had two corresponding stacks, one on the sending (you) node and the other on the receiving (your aunt) node. Also recall that the tasks in each protocol in the stack were based on a set of guidelines.

Now consider the same communication in a computer communication network. Suppose now that your aunt has a computer together with an e-mail account and instead of writing a snail mail as you previously did, you want to be modern and e-mail. The process, from the start on your side to the finish on your aunt's side, would go as follows.

You would start your computer, load your mail program, type your message and include in your e-mail your aunt's e-mail address, something like auntKay@something.tk. Upon submission of your e-mail, your client's e-mail software will try to talk to your server as it tries to send your e-mail to the server that will deliver it to your aunt, just like you took your letter to your mailbox in the postal system. Upon acceptance of your e-mail, your server will try to locate your aunt's server in domain .tk. We have left out lots of details which we will come back to later. After locating your aunt's server, your server will then forward your e-mail to it. Your aunt's server will then store the mail in your aunt's mail folder waiting for her computer to fetch it for her. The trail of this e-mail from the time it left your computer to the time it arrived in your aunt's mail folder consists of sets of activity groups we called stations in the postal system. The electronic version of these stations we will call *layers*. Again, like in the postal communication system, activities in each layer are performed based on a set of operational procedures we will also call *protocols*. In networking, protocols are like algorithms in mathematical computations. Algorithms spell out logical sequences of instructions for the computations and of course hide the details. Protocols do a similar thing in networking, providing hidden (from the user) logical sequences of detailed instructions. Broadly, these instructions make the source element initiate a communication, providing the identity of the destination and providing assurances that the intended destination will accept the message before any further communication is called for; and provide agreed on schemes to the destination element for translating and file management once the message is received.

These instructions call for a dual layered set of instructions we have called protocol stacks.

To streamline network communication, the International Standards Organization (ISO) developed the Open System Interconnection (OSI) model. The OSI is an open architecture model that functions as the network communication protocol standard, although it is not the most widely used. The TCP/IP (Transmission Control Protocol/Internet Protocol) protocol suite is the most widely used. Both OSI and TCP/IP models, like the postal system, use two protocol stacks, one at the source element and the other at the destination element

The development of the OSI model was based on the secure premise, like the postal communication system, that different layers of protocol provide different services and that each layer can communicate with only its own neighboring layers. That is, the protocols in each layer are based on the protocols of the previous layers. Figure 1.23 shows an OSI model consisting of seven layers and the descriptions of the services provided in each layer.

Layer	Description
Application	The interface between the user and all network application software
Presentation	Responsible for message syntax, conversions, compression, and encryption.
Session	Responsible for the organization and synchronization of source and destination during a communication session
Transport	Determines the class of service necessary for communication over the network. Among the classes are the connection oriented and the connectionless.
Network	This is responsible for mainly routing messages in the network from source to destination.
Data link	Responsible for acknowledging and retransmitting frames as an error control. It also controls the amount and speed of transmission on the network.
Physical	Responsible for placing bits on the transmission medium and has protocols that make all connectors and adaptors work.

Figure 1.23 OSI Protocol Layers and Corresponding Services

Figure 1.24 shows a logical communication model between you and your aunt using the OSI model. Although the development of the OSI model was intended to offer a standard for all other proprietary models, and it was as encompassing of all existing models as possible, it never really replaced many of those rival models it was intended to replace. In fact it is this "all in one" concept that caused its market failure because it became too complex. And its late arrival on the market also prevented its much anticipated interoperability across networks. Among OSI rivals was the TCP/IP which was far less complex and more historically established by the time the OSI came on the market. We will look at this next. Let us now focus on the TCP/IP model.

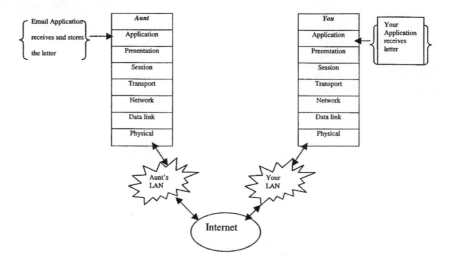

Figure 1.24 OSI Logical Model Connection

An Example of a Computer Communication Network Using TCP/IP: The Internet

The Internet is a network of communicating computing elements that uses a TCP/IP interoperability network model which is far less complex than the OSI model. The TCP/IP model is an evolving model with changing requirements as the Internet grows.

The Internet had its humble beginning from the research to develop a packet switching network funded by the Advanced Research Projects Agency (ARPA) of the Department of Defense (DOD). The resulting network was of course named ARPANET. TCP/IP is a protocol suite consisting of details of how computers should communicate, convey internetworking, and route traffic on computer networks. Like the OSI model, TCP/IP uses layered protocol stacks. These layers are: Application, Transport, Network, Data Link, and Physical. Figure 1.25 shows an Internet protocol stack of these layers.

However, whereas the OSI model uses seven layers as shown in Figure 1.23, the TCP/IP model uses five. Figure 1.26 shows the differences in layering between the OSI and TCP/IP models.

Layer	Delivery Unit	Protocols
Application	Message	File Transfer Protocol (FTP), Name Server Protocol (NSP), Simple Mail Transfer Protocol (SMTP), Simple Network Management Protocol (SNMP), HTTP, Remote file access (telnet), Network file system(NFS), Name Resolution (DNS)
Transport	Segment	Transmission Control Protocol (TCP), User Datagram Protocol (UDP).
Network	Datagram	Internet Protocol (IP), Internet Control Message Protocol (ICMP), Internet Group Management Protocol (IGMP).
Data Link	Frame	CSMA/CD for Ethernet and Token Ring
Physical	Bit Stream	All network card drivers.

Figure 1.25 TCP/IP Protocol Stacks

OSI - Layer	TCP/IP Layer	Protocols
Application	Application	File Transfer Protocol (FTP), Name Server Protocol (NSP), Simple Mail Transfer Protocol (SMTP), Simple Network Management Protocol (SNMP), HTTP, Remote file access (telnet), Network file system(NFS), Name Resolution (DNS)
Presentation		-
Session		-
Transport	Transport	Transmission Control Protocol (TCP), User Datagram Protocol (UDP).
Network	Network	Internet Protocol (IP), Internet Control Message Protocol (ICMP), Internet Group Management Protocol (IGMP).
Data Link	Data Link	CSMA/CD for Ethernet and Token Ring
Physical	Physical	All network card drivers.

Figure 1.26 OSI and TCP/IP Protocol Layers

Application Layer

This layer provides the user interface with resources rich in application functions. It supports all network applications and includes many protocols such as HTTP for web page access, SMTP for electronic mail, telnet for remote login, and FTP for file transfers. In addition, it provides Name Server Protocols (NSP) and Simple Network Management Protocol (SNMP), remote file server (telnet), and Domain Name Resolution Protocol (DNRP). Figure 1.27 shows an Application Layer data frame.

Application header protocols	Bit stream

Figure 1.27 Application Layer Data Frame

Transport Layer

This layer is a little bit removed from the user and it is hidden from the user. Its main purpose is to transport Application Layer messages that include Application Layer protocols in their headers between the host and the server. For the Internet network, the Transport Layer has two standard protocols: Transport Control Protocol (TCP) and User Datagram Protocol (UDP). TCP provides a connection-oriented service and it guarantees delivery of all application layer packets to their destination. This guarantee is based on two mechanisms: congestion control which throttles the transmission rate of the source element when there is traffic congestion in the network, and the flow control mechanism that tries to match sender and receiver speeds to synchronize the flow rate and reduce the packet drop rate. While TCP offers guarantees of delivery of the Application Layer packets, UDP on the other hand offers no such guarantees. It provides a no frills connectionless service with just delivery and no acknowledgments. But it is much more efficient and a protocol of choice for real-time data like streaming video and music. Transport Layer delivers transport layer packets and protocols to the Network Layer. Figure 1.28 shows the TCP data structure and Figure 1.29 shows the UDP data structure.

◄──────────────── ►32 bits◄ ────────────────►

Source address	Destination address
Sequence number	Acknowledgement number
Other control information	
Data	

Figure 1.28 TCP Structure

◄──────────────── ►32 bits◄ ────────────────►

Source address	Destination address
Other header control information	UDP Checksum
Data	

Figure 1.29 The UDP Structure

Network Layer

This layer moves packets, now called datagrams, from router to router along the path from a source host to the destination host. It supports a number of protocols including the Internet Protocol (IP), Internet Control Message Protocol (ICMP) and Internet Group Management Protocol (IGMP). The IP protocol is the most widely used Network Layer protocol. IP uses header information from the Transport Layer protocols that include datagram source and destination port numbers from IP-addresses, and other TCP header and IP information, to move datagrams from router to router through the network. Best routes are found in the network by using routing algorithms. Figure 1.30 shows an IP datagram structure.

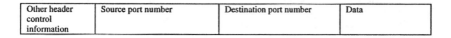

Other header control information	Source port number	Destination port number	Data

Figure 1.30 IP Datagram Structure

The standard IP-address has been the so-called IPv4, a 32-bit addressing scheme. But with the rapid growth of the Internet, there was fear of running out of addresses, so a new IPv6, a 64-bit addressing scheme, was created. The Network Layer conveys the network layer protocols to the Data Link Layer.

Data Link Layer

This layer provides the network with services that move packets from one packet switch like a router to the next over connecting links. This layer also offers reliable delivery of Network Layer packets over links. It is at the lowest level of communication and it includes the network interface card (NIC) and operating system (OS) protocols. The list of protocols in this layer include: Ethernet, ATM, and others like frame relay. Data Link Layer protocol unit, the frame, may be moved over links from source to destination by different link layer protocols at different links along the way.

Physical Layer

This layer is responsible for literally moving Data Link datagrams bit by bit over the links and between network elements. The protocols here depend on and use the characteristics of the link medium and the signals on the medium.

We have so far developed two parallel and strikingly similar communication models, the postal and computer communication network systems. Figure 1.31 gives parallel steps in both communication systems during a communication session. These scenarios were chosen because they represent the bulk of communication in the two systems. Mail communication is predominant in the postal system and forms a major part in the computer communication network system. Since the Internet uses the TCP/IP model, for the remainder of this book, as we discuss computer network security and issues of cyberspace attack that include causes, types, costs, and methods and techniques to combat such attacks and ensure cyberspace security, we will use the TCP/IP model as discussed in this chapter and illustrated in Figure 1.31 below.

Postal System Model

1. You write a letter, put it in an envelope add Aunt's address and your address.
2. Take letter to mailbox or Post Office.
3. Mail carrier collects letter
4. Letter put in car and taken to sorting center.
5. Letter sorted and grouped and moved to destination.
6. Abstraction of letter movement.
7. Receiving Post Office gets letter, sorts letter ready to deliver.
8. Mail carrier delivers to mailbox or puts in a letter box.
9. Someone retrieves letter from mailbox to Aunt.
10. Aunt opens and reads letter.

TCP/IP Model

1. Your computer SMTP mail client loads and prepares your email. It breaks the message into segments, puts source and destination addresses in each segment. (SMTP- Application)
2. Your computer, on LAN, initiates a three-way handshake as it broadcasts your message to the server. Local TCP adds sequence numbers to segments and sends segments to server. (TCP connection)
3. Server, after three-way handshake, receives segments, assigns acknowledgement numbers and buffers the segments. (TCP)
4. Server SMTP opens up initial connection with Aunt's server to agree on mail format and encoding of the message (SMTP –Application)
5. IP on server adds header control information to each segment to form datagrams ready for transportation. (IP).
6. Abstraction of datagram movement on the network mesh.
7. Aunt's server receives datagrams – using sequence numbers, buffers the datagrams, (TCP)
8. Aunt's computer makes a three-way handshake connection, SMTP on computer requests for mail from server.
9. Server SMTP, using agreed on format and encoding reassembles the message. Server TCP segments the message and assigns sequence numbers to each segment and sends segment to client. (TCP)
10. Aunt's computer receives segments, SMTP reassembles message and loads it and Aunt reads it.

Figure 1.31 Comparison of TCP/IP and Postal System Communication Models

Chapter 2

Anatomy of the Problem

*You have to do something to raise their level of awareness
that they cannot be victims....* — Kevin Mitnick

The recent computer security breaches that included the much debated distributed denial of service attacks (DDoS), some of which have been attributed to a Canadian teen masquerading in cyberspace as "Mafiaboy," the Manila-generated "Love Bug," and the "Killer Resume" e-mail attacks that wreaked havoc on world computer networks, were, in addition to being attention-grabbing headlines, loud wake-up bells. Not only did these incidents expose law enforcement agencies' lack of expertise in digital forensics, they also alerted a complacent society to the weaknesses in the computer network infrastructure, the poor state of the nation's computer security preparedness, the little knowledge many of us have about computer security and the lack of efforts to secure computer systems' infrastructure [1, 2]. They also highlighted the vulnerability of cyberspace businesses including critical national infrastructures like power grids, water systems, financial institutions, communication systems, energy, public safety, and all other systems run by computers that foreign governments or cyber-terrorists could attack via the Internet.

In fact the Love Bug's near lightning strike of global computers, its capacity to penetrate the world's powerful government institutions with impunity, though by its very origin very unsophisticated, and the easy and rapid spread of the Killer Resume virus, although it attacked during off-peak hours, show how easy it is to bring the world's computer infrastructure and all that depend on it to a screeching stop. They also demonstrate how the world's computer networks are at the mercy of not only the affluent pre-teens and teens, as in the case of the Mafiaboy, but also of the not so affluent people, as in the case of the Philippines Love Bug creator. With national critical systems on the line, sabotage should no longer be expected to come from only known high-tech and rich countries but from anywhere, the ghettos of Manila and the jungles of the Amazon included.

As computer know-how and use spreads around the world, so do the dangers of computer attacks. How on earth did we come to this point? We are a smart people that designed the computer, constructed the computer communication network, developed the protocols to support computer communication, yet we cannot safeguard any of these jewels from attacks, misuse, and abuse. One explanation might be rooted in the security flaws that exist in the computer communication network infrastructures, especially the Internet. Additional explanations might be: users' and system administrators' limited knowledge of the infrastructure, society's increasing dependence on a system whose infrastructure and technology it least understands, lack of long-term plans and mechanisms in place or planned to educate the public, a highly complacent society which still accords a "whiz kid" status to cyber vandals, inadequate security mechanisms and solutions often involving no more than patching loopholes after an attack has occurred, lack of knowledge concerning the price of this escalating problem (a lack that so far there has been no concrete effort to correct), the absence of mechanisms to enforce reporting of computer crimes (which is as of now voluntary, sporadic, and haphazard), and the fact that the nation is yet to understand the seriousness of cyber vandalism. A detailed discussion of these explanations follows.

Computer Network Infrastructure Weaknesses and Vulnerabilities

The cyberspace infrastructure, as we studied it in Chapter 1, was developed not following a well conceived and understood plan with clear blueprints, but it was developed in steps in reaction to the changing needs of a developing intra and inter communication between computing elements. The hardware infrastructure and corresponding underlying protocols suffer from weak points and sometimes gaping loopholes partly as a result of the infrastructure open architecture protocol policy. This policy, coupled with the spirit of individualism and adventurism, gave birth to the computer industry and underscored the rapid, and sometimes motivated, growth of the Internet. However, the same policy acting as a magnet has attracted all sorts of people to develop exploits for the network's vulnerable and weak points, in search of a challenge, adventurism, fun, and all forms of personal fulfillments.

Compounding the problem of open architecture is the nature and the working of the communication protocols. The Internet as a packet network works by breaking data, to be transmitted into small individually addressed packets that are downloaded on the network's mesh of switching elements. Each individual packet finds its way through the network with no predetermined route and is used in the reassembling of the message by the receiving element. Packet networks need a strong trust relationship that must exist among the transmitting elements. Such a relationship is actually supported by the communication protocols. Let us see how this is done.

Computer communicating elements have almost the same etiquettes like us, for example, if you want a service performed for you by a stranger, you first establish a relationship with the stranger. This can be done in a number of ways. Some people start with a formal "Hello, I'm ...," then, "I need ..." upon which the stranger says "Hello, I'm ..." then, " Sure I can...." Others carry it further to hugs, kisses, and all other techniques people use to break the ice. If the stranger is ready to do business with you, then this information is passed back to you in a form of an acknowledgment to your first embraces. However, if the stranger is not ready to talk to you, there is usually no acknowledgment to your initial advances and no further communication may follow until the stranger's acknowledgment comes through. At this point the stranger puts out a welcome mat and leaves the door open for you to come in and start business. Now it is up to the initiator of the communication to start full communication.

When computers are communicating they follow these etiquette patterns and protocols and we call this procedure a handshake. In fact for computers it is called a three way handshake. A three-way handshake, briefly discussed in Chapter 1, starts with the client sending a packet, called a SYN (short for synchronization), which contains both the client and server addresses together with some initial information for introductions. Upon receipt of this packet by the server's welcome open door called a *port*, the server creates a communication socket with the same port number like the client requested through which future communication with the client will go. After creating the communication socket, the server puts the socket in queue and informs the client by sending an acknowledgment called a SYN-ACK. The server's communication socket will remain open and in queue waiting for an ACK from the client and data packets thereafter. As long as the communication socket remains open and as long as the client remains silent, not sending in an ACK, the communication socket is *half open* and it remains in the queue in the server memory. During this time, however, the server can welcome many more clients that want to communicate, and communication sockets will be opened for each. If any of their corresponding clients do not send in the ACK, their sockets will remain half open and also queued. Queued half open sockets can stay in the queue for a specific time interval after which they are purged. Figure 2.1 below shows a three-way handshake.

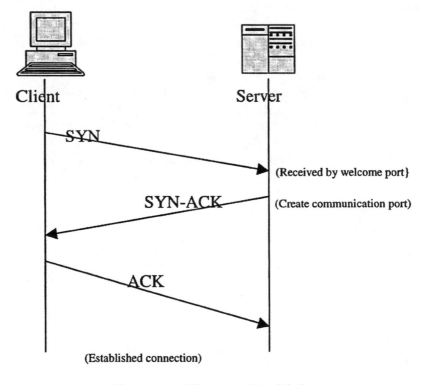

Figure 2.1 A Three-way Handshake

The three-way handshake establishes a trust relationship between the sending and receiving elements. However, network security exploits that go after infrastructure and protocol loopholes do so by targeting to undermine this trust relationship created by the three-way handshake. A discussion of the infrastructure protocol exploits and other operating system specific attacks follows.

TCP/IP and UDP Protocols

IP-Spoofing

Internet Protocol spoofing (IP-spoofing) is a technique used to set up an attack on computer network communicating elements by altering the IP addresses of the source element in the data packets replacing them with bogus addresses. IP-spoofing creates a situation that breaks down the normal trust-relationship that should exist between two communicating elements. IP, as we saw in Chapter 1, is the connectionless, unreliable network protocol in the TCP/IP suite charged with routing packets around the network. In doing its job, IP simply sends out datagrams (data packets) with a hope that, with luck, the datagrams will make it to the destination intact. If the datagrams do not make it all the way to the destination, IP sends an error message back to the sending element to inform it of the loss. However, IP does not even guarantee that the error message will arrive to the sending element. In fact IP does not have any knowledge of the connection state of any of the datagrams it has been entrusted with to route through the network. In addition IP's datagrams are quite easy to open and take a look at and modify at will to allow an arbitrarily chosen IP address to be inserted in a datagram as a legitimate source address.

These conditions set the stage for IP spoofing by allowing a small number of true IP addresses to be used bogusly by a large number of communicating elements. The process works as follows: one communicating element intercepts IP datagrams, opens them and modifies their source IP-addresses and forwards them on. Any other switching element in the network that gets any of these datagrams maps these addresses in its table as legal source IP-addresses, and uses them for further correspondence with the "source" elements with those bogus addresses. IP-spoofing, as we will soon see, is a basic ingredient in many types of network attacks.

SYN Flooding

SYN flooding is an attack that utilizes the break down in the trust relationship between two or more communicating elements to overwhelm the resources of the targeted element by sending huge volumes of spoofed packets. SYN flooding works as follows. Recall from above that when a client attempts to establish a TCP connection to a server, the client and server first exchange packets of data in a three-way handshake. The three-way handshake creates a half-open connection while the server is waiting for an ACK packet from the client. During this time, however, other communicating elements may start their own three-way handshakes. If none of the clients send in their respective ACK, the server queue of half open connection sockets may grow beyond the server system memory capacity and thus create a memory overflow. When a server memory overflow occurs, a couple of things happen to the server; in the first instance, the server table grows huge and for each new SYN request, it takes a lot of time for the server to search the table, thus increasing the system response time. Also as the response time increasingly grows and as the buffer fills up, the server starts to drop all new packets directed to it. This server state can be maliciously brought about intentionally by selecting a victim server and bombarding it with thousands of SYN packets each with what appears to be legitimate source IP addresses, thus flooding it with SYN packets. However, these are usually bogus IP-addresses with no existing client to respond to the server with an ACK. Although the queued half-open connections have a time slice quantum limit beyond which they are automatically removed from the queue, if the rate at which new incoming SYN connections are made is higher than the rate the half-open connections are removed from the queue, then the server may start to limp. If the attacking clients simply continue sending IP-spoofed packets, the victim server will succumb to the avalanche and crush. Figure 2.2 on page 43 shows a TCP SYN flooding. SYN flooding does not only affect one victim server, its effects on one server may ripple through the network creating secondary and subsequent victims.

Secondary and subsequent victims are created by making source IP-addresses appear to come from legitimate domains whose addresses are in the global routing tables. Those legitimate machines with forged IP-addresses become secondary victims because the first victim server sends to them SYN-ACKs for which they have no idea. The victims may reply to the unsolicited SYN-ACKs by themselves sending the ACK to the victim server, therefore, becoming victims themselves.

Sequence Numbers Attack

Two of the most important fields of a TCP datagram shown in Figure 2.3 are the sequence number and acknowledgment field. The fields are filled in by the sending and receiving elements during a communication session. Let us see how this is done. Suppose client A wants to send 200 bytes of data to server B using 2-byte TCP packets. The packets A will send to B will be as shown in Figure 2.3 on page 43.

The first packet A will send to B will have two bytes, byte 0 and byte 1, and will have a sequence number 0. The second packet will have bytes 2 and 3 and will be assigned sequence number 2. Note that the sequence number

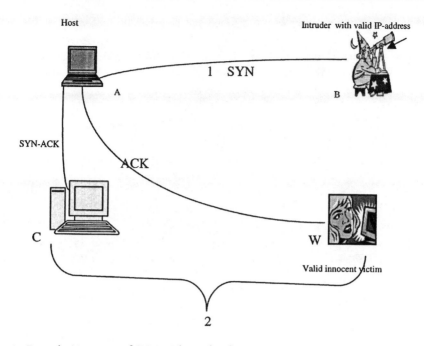

1. B sends A streams of SYN with randomly changing source addresses from valid IP-class addresses.
2. A sends a stream of SYN-ACK to each valid addressed SYN — these are sent to hosts with no knowledge of what is going on and have no involvement in the attack. These victims have no addresses in the global Internet routing tables, therefore, they are not reachable.

Figure 2.2 TCP SYN Flooding

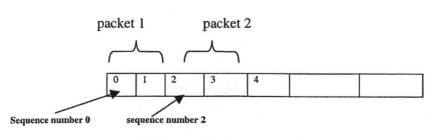

Figure 2.3 TCP Datagram

is not the byte number but the first byte number in each packet. Upon receipt of the packets from A, B will send acknowledgments to A with an acknowledgment number. Recall TCP is a full duplex communication protocol, meaning that during any communication session, there is a simultaneous two-way communication session during which A and B can talk to each other without one waiting for the other to finish before it can start. B acknowledges A's packets by informing A of the receipt of all the packets except the missing ones. So in this case B sends an ACK packet with an acknowledgment number and its own sequence number, which is the next number to the last sequence number it has received. For example, suppose A has sent packets with sequence numbers 0, 1, 2, ... 15, B will send an acknowledgment of these packets through sequence number 15 with acknowledgment number 16. Figure 2.4 shows a structure of a TCP connection session packet; and Figure 2.5 shows a TCP connection session using sequence numbers (SNs) and acknowledgment numbers (ACNs).

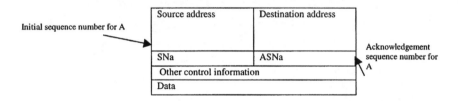

Figure 2.4 TCP Connection Session Packet Structure

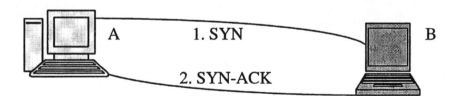

1. A SYN (ISNa — initial sequence number a)— A sends a first packet to B with initial sequence number a.
2. B replies to A with ACK (SNb, SNa), two sequence numbers, its own sequence number (SNb) and acknowledging the sent number (SNa).

Figure 2.5 A TCP Connection Session

The initial sequence number (ISN) is supposed to be random and sub-sequent numbers are incremented by a constant based on time (usually seconds) and connection (RFC 793). The initial sequence number attack is a technique that allows an attacker to create a one-way TCP connection with a target element while spoofing another element by guessing the TCP sequence numbers used. This is done by the attacker intercepting the communication session between two or more communicating elements and then guessing the next sequence number in a communication session. The intruder then slips the spoofed IP addresses into packets transmitted to the server. The server sends acknowledgment to the spoofed clients. Let us illustrate such an attack in Figure 2.6 below.

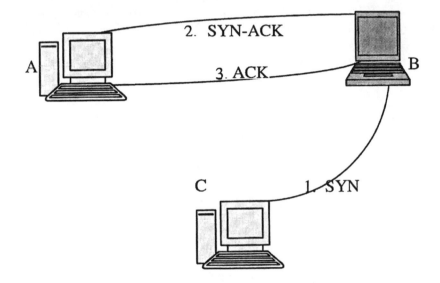

1. C, the attacker, opens a connection with B by sending (SYN, ISNa) masquerading as A, where ISNa is the initial sequence number for A
2. B responds by sending a SYN-ACK to A (ACK, ISNb, ISNa).
3. A acknowledges B by sending ACK (ISNa, ISNb). Although A does NOT know anything about the SYN to B, it responds anyway by using the guessed ISNb.
4. B now believes it has a legitimate session with A. However C, the intruder, is actually communicating with B.

Figure 2.6 Initial Sequence Number Attack

However, it is possible for client A to realize that server B is actually acknowledging a packet that A did not send in the first place. In this case A may send a request (RST) to B to bring down the connection. However, this is possible if A is not kept busy, and this is where the exploit is. The trick is to send a smurf attack on A to keep A as busy as possible so that it does not have time to respond to B with an RST. In this case then, the intruder successfully becomes a legitimate session member with server B.

Scanning and Probing Attacks

In scanning and probing attack, the intruder or intruders send large quantities of packets from a single location. The activity involves mostly a Trojan horse remote controlled program with a distributed scanning engine that is configured to scan carefully selected ports. Currently the most popular ports are port 80, used by World Wide Web applications, port 8080, used by World Wide Web proxy services, and port 3128, used by most common squid proxy services.

Low Bandwidth Attacks

A low-bandwidth attack starts by sending a low volume, intermittent series of scanning or probing packets from various locations. The attack may involve several hackers from different locations all concurrently scanning and probing the network for vulnerabilities. Low-bandwidth attacks can involve as few as five to 10 packets per hour, from as many different sources.

Session Attacks

Many other types of attacks are targeted not at the break down of the three-way handshake relationship. There are a number of attacks that target sessions already in progress and break into such sessions. Let us look at several of these, namely packet sniffing, buffer overflow, and session hijacking.

A *packet sniffer* is a program on a network element connected to a network to passively receive all Data Link Layer frames passing through the device's network interface. This potentially makes all hosts connected to the network a possible packet sniffer. If host A is transmitting to host B and there is a packet sniffer in the communication path between them, then all data frames sent from A to B and vice versa are "sniffed." A sniffed frame can have its content, message, and header altered, modified, even deleted and replaced. For example, in a network element in a local area network (LAN) with Ethernet protocols, if the network card is set to promiscuous mode, the interface can be able to receive all passing frames. The intercepted frames are then passed over to the Application Layer program to extract any type of data the intruder may have an interest in. Figure 2.7 shows how packet sniffing works.

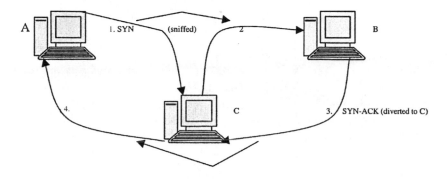

1. A sends a SYN packet to B for login containing source and destination address and password.
2. C, the intruder, sniffs the packet A is sending to B and gets A's and B's address and A's password to B.
3. B, with no knowledge of C in the middle, sends a SYN-ACK and permission to enter which is directed to C.
4. C is now in full access to both A and B after sniffing the SYN-ACK.

Figure 2.7 Packet Sniffing

A *buffer overflow* is an attack that allows the intruder to overrun one or more program variables thus making it easy for an intruder to execute arbitrary codes with the privilege of the current user. Intruders usually target the root (highest privileged user on the system). The problem is always a result of bad program coding. Such coding may include a program that lacks good string or buffer data types in C, misuse of standard C library string functions, and if buffers are used, not being able to check the size of the buffer whenever data is inserted in the buffer. In a network environment, especially a UNIX environment, buffer overflow can create serious security problems because an attacker can, from anywhere, execute an attack on a system of choice.

Session hijacking may occur in several situations. For example, quite often clients may desire services, like software stored at a server. In order to access such services, the server may require the client to send authenticating information that may include a password and username. In some cases, especially where requests from a client are frequent, the server may store the user ID with the access URL so that the server can quickly recognize the "returning" user without going through an authentication exercise every time a request comes from this client. Thus a trust relationship is established. By so doing, the server automatically opens up loopholes through which an intruder, after sniffing the legitimate source IP address, can hijack a server TCP session without the knowledge of both the server and client. A more common type of session hijacking is for the intruder to become a legal participant by monitoring a session between two communicating hosts and then injecting traffic that appears to be coming from those hosts. Eventually one of the legitimate hosts is dropped, thus making the intruder legitimate. Yet another type is referred to as *"blind" hijacking* whereby an intruder can guess the responses of the two communicating elements, thus becoming a fully trusted participant without the intruder seeing the responses.

Session hijacking can take place even if the targeted communication element rejects the source IP address packets. This is possible if the initial connection sequence numbers can be predicted. Figure 2.8 on page 49 illustrates a typical session hijacking using initial connection sequence numbers (ISN).

Distributed Denial of Service Attacks (DDoS)

Distributed denial of service (DDoS) attacks are generally classified as nuisance attacks in the sense that they simply interrupt the services of the system. System interruption can be as serious as destroying a computer's hard disk or as simple as using up all the system available memory. DDoS come in many forms but the most common are the following:

Ping of Death

The Ping of Death is one of several possible ICMP Protocol attacks. The Internet Control Message Protocol (ICMP) is an IP protocol used in the exchange of messages. The IP-datagram encapsulates the ICMP message as shown in Figure 2.9 on page 49.

According to RFC-791, an IP packet including those containing ICMP messages can be as long as 65,353 (2^{16-1}) octets. An octet is a group of eight items. When packets are bigger than the maximum allowable IP packet structure, such packets are fragmented into smaller products. ICMP ECHO_REQUESTs are called pings. Normal network pings, as we have seen before, are done by the server broadcasting ICMP ECHO_REQUEST packets every

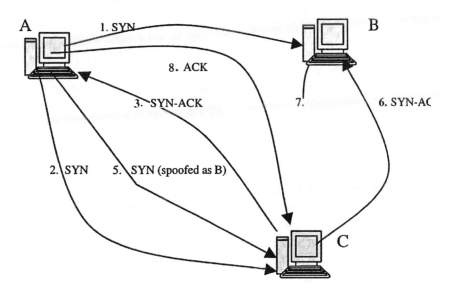

1. A sends a SYN flood to B — to keep it busy.
2. A also SYN to C.
3. C returns a SYN-ACK to A with (initial sequence numbers (ISN).
4. C increments the ISN for this connection (a process, not on figure).
5. A then SYN to C spoofed as B (recall B is busy).
6. C sends a SYN-ACK to B and an ISN (which A captures).
7. But there is no response from B to C (it is SYN-flooded).
8. A sends an ACK to C masquerading as B containing the guessed ISN+1. If the guess is correct, then C believes A to be B and A has successfully hijacked C's session.

Figure 2.8 Session Hijacking Using Sequence Numbers

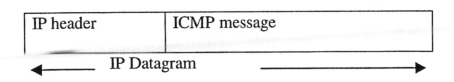

Figure 2.9 IP-ICMP Packet

second and waiting for a SIGALRM (short for signal alarm) packet signal from the clients. A ping flood occurs when the client sends lots of SIGALRM signals to the ping generator, in this case the server. The problem in this category is partly by the size of these SIGALRM packets. If the SIGALRM packets sent by the client to the server are large and are not fragmented into smaller packets, they can cause havoc. Large IP packets are known as "Ping of Death." You see, when packets get larger, the underlying protocols that handle them become less efficient. However, in normal data transmission, bigger than the maximum size IP packets are broken up into smaller packets which are then reassembled by the receiver.

Smurfing

The "smurf" attack also utilizes the broken down trust relationship created by IP-spoofing. An offending element sends a large amount of spoofed ping packets containing the victim's IP-address as the source address. Ping traffic, also called Protocol Overview Internet Control Message Protocol (ICMP) in the Internet community, is used to report out-of-band messages related to network operation or mis-operation such as a host or entire portion of the network being unreachable, due to some type of failure. The pings are then directed to a large number of network subnets, a subnet being a small independent network like a LAN. If all subnets reply to the victim address, the victim element receives a high rate of requests from the spoofed addresses as a result and the element begins buffering these packets. When the requests come at a rate exceeding the capacity of the queue, the element generates ICMP Source Quench messages meant to slow down the sending rate. These messages are then sent, supposedly, to the legitimate sender of the requests. If the sender is legitimate, it will heed to the requests and slow down the rate of packet transmission. However, in cases of spoofed addresses, no action is taken because all sender addresses are bogus. The situation in the network can easily deteriorate further if each routing device itself takes part in smurfing.

Teardrop Attack

This is an attack that exploits the fragmentation vulnerability mechanism of ICMP ECHO_REQUEST packets just like the Ping of Death attacks. However, the teardrop attacks work by attacking the re-assembling mechanism of the fragmented IP-packets resulting in overlapping fragments that often lead to targeted hosts to hang or crush altogether [3].

Land.c Attack

This attack is initiated by an intruder sending a TCP SYN packet giving the target host's addresses as both the source and destination addresses.

It also uses the host's port number on both the source and destination port numbers [3].

The techniques we have seen above are collectively known as denial of service attacks (DDoS). Any system connected to the Internet and using TCP and UDP protocol services like WWW, Mail, FTP, and telnet is potentially subject to this attack. The attack may be selectively targeted to specific communicating elements or it might be directed to randomly selected victims.

Although we seem to understand how the DDoS problems do arise, we have yet to come up with meaningful and effective solutions. What makes the search for a solution even more elusive is the fact that we cannot even notice that a server is under attack since the IP spoofing connection requests, for example, may not lead to a system overload. While the attack is going on, the system may still be able to function satisfactorily establishing outgoing connections. Which brings one to wonder how many such attacks are going on without ever being detected, and what fraction of those attacks are ever detected.

Network Operating Systems and Software Vulnerabilities

Network infrastructure exploits are not limited to protocols. There are weaknesses and loopholes in network software that include network operating systems, web browsers, and network applications. Such loopholes are quite often targets of hacker aggressive attacks like planting Trojan horse viruses, deliberately inserting backdoors, stealing sensitive information, and wiping out files from systems. Such exploits have become common. Let's look at some operating system vulnerabilities.

Windows NT and NT Registry Attacks

The Windows NT Registry is a central repository for all sensitive system and configuration information. It contains five permanent parts, called *hives*, to control local machine information that include booting and running the system, information on hardware configuration data, resource usage, per-machine software data, account and group databases, system-wide security policies that include hashed passwords, program locations, program default settings, lists of trusted systems, and audit settings, and performance counters. Almost all applications added to the NT machine and nearly all security settings affect the registry. The registry is a trove of information for attackers and it is a prime target for many computer attacks. Common NT Registry attacks include the L0pht Crack, the Chargen Attack, the SSP-ING/JOLT, and the RedButton.

The *L0pht Crack* works by guessing passwords on either the local or remote machine. Once the hacker has succeeded in guessing a password and gained entry, the hacker then makes bogus passwords and establishes new accounts. Now the attacker can even try to gain access to privileged access accounts.

The *Chargen Attack* is a malicious attack that may be mounted against computers running Windows NT and 2000. The attack consists of a flood of UDP datagrams sent to the subnet broadcast address with the destination port set to 19 (chargen) and a spoofed source IP address. The Windows NT and 2000 computers running Simple TCP/IP services respond to each broadcast, creating a flood of UDP datagrams, that eventually cripple a selected server.

The SSPING/JOLT is a version of the old SysV and Posix implementations. It effectively freezes almost any Windows95 or Windows NT connection by sending a series of spoofed and fragmented ICMP packets to the target. A server running Windows95/98/NT/2000 may crumble altogether. This is a version of the "Ping of Death" we saw earlier targeted on computers running Windows 95/98/NT/2000.

The *RedButton* allows an attacker of the NT Registry to bypass the traditional logon procedure that requires a valid username and password combination, or the use of a guest account. The bug grants that user access to intimate system information on an NT server without these requirements. It does this by exploiting an alternate means of access to an NT system using an anonymous account, which is normally used for machine-to-machine communication on a network. This anonymous account gives a successful attacker full access to all system resources available to an NT group named "everyone," that includes all system users.

UNIX

UNIX's source code, unlike Windows NT, has for a long time been publicly released and its many flaws have been widely discussed and of course exploited. This leads to the perception that Windows NT is actually more secure—a false assumption. In fact Windows NT has many of UNIX's flaws.

There are many other types of proprietary operating system attacks and Table 2.1 below lists some of the most known.

Attack name	Operating system	Description of attack
Tribe and Trinoo	Solaris/Linux	Attacks files /DDoS
Tribe flood Network	Solaris/Linux	Attacks files/DDoS
TFN2K	Solaris/Linux	Attacks files/DDoS
Core-dump	NT/2000	Attacks the root via the /tmp sub-directory
MS-Office 7.0	NT/2000	Attacks MS files
CPU attacks	NT/2000	Attacks CPU using telnet
MS Word Excel	NT/2000	Attacks MS Excel files
Love Bug	NT/2000	E-mail attachments
Killer Resume	NT/2000	E-mail attachments
Melissa	95/98/NT	E-mail attachments
NT Registry	NT/2000	Attacks NT registry
Win32K Crash	95/98/NT	Attacks Windows Kernel

Table 2.1 Proprietary Operating System Exploits

Limited Knowledge of Users and System Administrators

The limited knowledge computer users and system administrators have about computer network infrastructure and the working of its protocols does not help advance network security. In fact it increases the dangers. In a mechanical world where users understand the systems, things work differently. For example in a mechanical system like a car, if such a car has fundamental mechanical weaknesses, the driver usually understands and finds those weak points and repairs them. This, however, is not the case with computer networks. As we have seen, the network infrastructure has weaknesses and this situation is complicated when both system administrators and users have limited knowledge of how the system works, its weaknesses and when such weaknesses are in the network. This lack of knowledge leads to other problems that further complicate network security. Among such factors are the following:

- Network administrators do not use effective encryption schemes, and do not use or enforce a sound security policy.
- Less knowledgeable administrators and users quite often use blank or useless passwords, and they rarely care to change even the good ones.
- Users carelessly give away information to criminals without being aware of the security implications. For example Kevin Mitnick, a

notorious hacker, claims to have gotten access to the Motorola company computer network by persuading company employees to give up passwords on the pretext that he was one of them. This very example illustrates the enormous task of educating users to be more proactive as far as computer security is concerned.

- Network administrators fail to use system security filters. According to security experts, network servers without filters "are the rule rather than the exception."

Society's Dependence on Computers

All the problems we have discussed so far are happening at a time when computer and Internet use are on the rise. Computer dependency is increasing as computers increasingly become part of our everyday life. From Wall Street to private homes, dependency on computers and computer technology shows no signs of abating. As we get more and more entangled in a computer driven economy, very few in society have a sound working knowledge and understanding of the basics of how computers communicate and how their e-mail and Internet surfing work. Indeed, few show any interest in learning. This has always been the case with the technology we use every day. From the business point of view, technology works better and is embraced faster if all its complexities are transparent to the user, and therefore, user-friendly. Few of us bother to learn much about cars, television, washers and dryers, or even faucets and drains, because when they break down and need fixing we always call in a mechanic, a technician, or a plumber! What is so different about computers and computer networks?

What is different is the enormous amount of potential for abuse of computers and computer networks — and the possibility of damage over vast amounts of cyberspace.

Lack of Planning

Despite the potential for computer and computer network abuses to wreak havoc on our computer dependent society, as demonstrated by the "Love Bug" and the "Killer Resume" bug, there are few signs that we are getting the message and making plans to educate the populace on computer use and security. Beside calling on the FBI to hunt abusers down, apprehend them, bring them to book with the stiffest jail sentences to send a signal to other would-bes, and demanding for tougher laws, there is nothing on the horizon. There is no clear plan or direction, no blueprint to guide the national efforts in finding a solution; very little has been done on the education front.

Complacent Society

When the general public holds some specialty in high regard, usually it is because the public has little knowledge of that specialty. The less knowledge we possess in some field, the more status we accord to those whose knowledge is great. I have little knowledge of how satellites can be guided in the emptiness of space and land on an outer space object, in a specific pre-selected spot millions of miles away, so I really respect space scientists. However, when my bathroom faucet leaks, I can fix it in a few hours; therefore, I do not have as much respect for plumbers as I do for space scientists.

The same reasoning applies to computer users concerning computers and how they work. The public still accords "whiz kid" status to computer vandals. Do we accord them that status because they are young and computer literate and few of us used computers at their age, or because we think that they are smarter than we are? Not only do we admire the little vandals, we seem mesmerized with them and their actions do not seem to register on the radar, at least not yet. This is frightening, to say the least.

Inadequate Security Mechanism and Solutions

Although computer network software developers and hardware manufacturers have tried to find solutions to the network infrastructure and related problems, sound and effective solutions are yet to be found. In fact all solutions that have been provided so far by both hardware and software manufacturers have been not really solutions but patches. For example when the distributed denial of service (DDoS) attack occurred, Cisco, one of the leading network router manufacturers, immediately, through its vendors, issued patches as solutions to DDoS attacks. This was followed by IBM, another leading router manufacturer; a few others followed the examples of the industry leaders. More recently, when both the Manila "Love Bug" and the "Killer Resume" bugs struck e-mail applications on global networks, Microsoft, the developer of Outlook, which was the main conduit of both bugs, immediately issued a patch. These are not isolated incidents but a pattern in the two computer industry's major component manufacturers.

A computer communication network is only as good as its weakest hardware link and its poorest network protocol. In fact infrastructure attacks like those outlined above have no known fixes. For example there is no known effective defense against denial of service attacks. Several hardware manufacturers of network infrastructure items like routers and other switches have, in addition to offering patches, recommended to their customers to boost the use of filters. Few of these remedies have worked effectively so far.

These best known security mechanisms and solutions, actually half solutions to the network infrastructure problems, are inadequate at best. More effective solutions to the network protocol weaknesses are not in sight. This, together with the lack of apprehending the perpetrators like those in the recent denial of service attacks by the FBI and other law enforcement agencies highlight an urgent need for a solution that is still elusive. Yet the rate of such crimes is on the rise as the data from CERT [5] in the graph in Figure 2.10 below indicates. With such rise, the law enforcement agencies are not able to cope with the rising epidemic as they lack both technical know-how and capacity. Michael Vatis, director of the FBI's National Infrastructure Protection Center, testifies to this when he says that due to limited capacity, attacks like spoofing make it very difficult for the law enforcement to determine where an attack originates from [5].

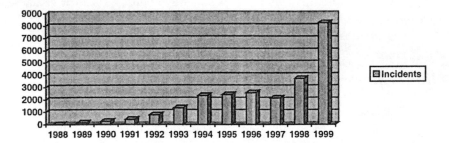

Figure 2.10 Graph Indicating the Rising Incidents of Computer Attacks

This explains why the FBI took so long to apprehend the recent cyber vandals like the DDoS attacks, and the circus-like atmosphere in the attempted arrest of the authors of the "Love Bug" in Manila. Vatis, like many, sees no immediate solution from both the technology and the FBI and he proposes two possible solutions:

(i)   enabling civilians not bound by the Fourth Amendment to conduct investigations and

(ii) somehow defeating spoofing with better technology. None of his solutions is yet feasible.

Poor Reporting of Computer Crimes

Meanwhile headline-making vandals keep on striking, making more and more daring acts with impunity. Along with those headline makers, there are thousands of others not reported. The number of reported cyber crimes tracked by CERT, the FBI, and local enforcement authorities is low. In fact according to reports, two-thirds of computer firms do not report hacker attacks [6]. According to the U.S. Senate report on security in cyberspace, many government departments, including Defense, have no mandatory reporting [7]. It is even worse when it comes to detection and intrusion. According to the same report, using the 1996 statistics of the Defense Information Systems Agency (DISA), an agency that performs proactive vulnerability assessment of the Defense Department computer networks, of the 18,200 systems DISA penetrated, only five percent of those intrusions were detected by system administrators. And of the 910 systems users that detected the intrusions, only 27 percent reported such intrusions to their superiors [7].

Similar numbers are probably found in the private sector. In a study by the Computer Security Institute (CSI), of the 4,971 questionnaires sent to Information Security practitioners, seeking information on system intrusions, only 8.6 percent responded. Even those few responding, only 42 percent admitted that intrusions ever occurred in their systems [7]. This low reporting rate can be attributed to a number of reasons including the following:

- Many of those who would have liked to report such crimes do not do so because of both economic and a psychological impact such news would have on both the shareholders' confidence and the overall name of the company. Lack of customer confidence is a competitor's advantage and it may spell financial ruin to the company. Some companies are reluctant to report any form of computer attacks on their systems in fear that others, including shareholders, will perceive company management as weak with poor security policies.
- There is little to no interest in reporting.
- The law enforcement agencies, especially the FBI, do not have highly specialized personnel to effectively track down the intruders. Even those few are overworked and underpaid according to the ABC report [6].
- Companies and businesses hit by cyber vandalism have little faith in the law enforcement agencies, especially the FBI, because they think the FBI, in its present state and capacity, can do little. The burden

to catch and apprehend cyber criminals is still on the FBI. This explains why there has been slow progress in apprehending the recent perpetrators of the recent denial of service and "Love Bug" attacks,

The FBI's problems are perpetuated by the fact that the laws that would help the FBI speed up the search and apprehension processes have not kept up with technology. For example according to an ABC News report, the FBI cannot quickly and readily share evidence of viruses and attack programs they might stumble on with private companies that have the capacity and technical know-how. By the time private computer industry with the technical know-how gets hold of such evidence samples, according to federal grand jury evidence rules, the tracks left by the intruders have become cold.

The law enforcement situation becomes even more murky when it is on a global scale. The global mosaic of laws, political systems, and law enforcement capacity make badly needed global efforts even more unattainable. Yet, as the "Love Bug" e-mail attack demonstrated, computer attacks have become global. This is making the search for perpetrators even more difficult. The characteristic profile of a well-to-do Westerner as computer attacker has been shattered by the "Love Bug." Hackers can be anywhere, thanks to the miracles of modern technology. The FBI may have to search all the jungles of the Amazon and the Congo.

Also current wiretap laws were designed for lengthy surveillance in one place in order to build a case. And if there is a cause to track down a perpetrator, court orders must be sought in every judicial district, which takes time and may lead to evidence getting altered or destroyed altogether. However, cyber attacks that are quick and can instantaneously have a global reach cannot be monitored from one place, and evidence cannot wait for court orders. This problem was no better highlighted than in the attempted arrest of the authors of the "Love Bug." It took two days to even attempt to arrest a suspect because there were no computer crime laws on books in the Philippines. So the judge could not quickly issue an arrest warrant. National laws have to be amended to make it easier to pursue attackers. To be effective such laws must allow investigators, among other things, to completely trace an online communication to its source without seeking permission from each jurisdiction. More money must be allocated to hire prosecutors and analysts, as well as improving the research capability of all law enforcement agencies. In addition to these, there must be continuous training in the latest developments in digital forensics of those already in law enforcement agencies. If all these are put in place, then we will be on the way to making cyberspace safer for all.

Although network infrastructure weaknesses we have discussed in this chapter seem simple, finding a solution has not been easy and it is an ongoing exercise of interest to lawmakers, law enforcement agencies, and the network community. Although the Holy Grail is to find a final solution to the dreaded computer network security problems, whether we succeed or not, such a solution will not last long, for the following reasons:

- The cyberspace infrastructure technology is constantly changing, adding new technologies along the way, and as new technologies are added, new loopholes and, therefore, new opportunities are created for the cyber vandals.
- Solutions to social and ethical problems require a corresponding change in the legal structures, enforcement mechanisms, and human moral and ethical systems. None of these can change at the speed technology is changing. Pretty soon, any solution will be useless and we will be back to square one.
- As yet, there is no national or multinational plan or policy that can stand the rapid changes in technology and remain enforceable.
- Most importantly, solutions that do not take into account and are not part of a general public education plan do not stand a chance of lasting for any extended period of time. For any lasting solution to the computer network security problem, public education and awareness are critical.

A workable and durable solution, if found, must include the following:

- public awareness and understanding of the computer network infrastructure threats, its potential consequences and its vulnerabilities. We cannot rely on education acquired from science-fiction novels. Otherwise when such attacks really occur, the public may take them to be science-fiction events.
- a well-developed plan based on a good policy for deterrence.
- and a clear plan, again based on good and sound policy, for rapid and timely response to cyber attacks.

Chapter 3

Types of Cyber Attacks

*Cybercrimes and other information-security breaches are
widespread and diverse.* — Patrice Rapalus, director
of the Computer Security Institute

While Gibson's vision of cyberspace, as discussed in Chapter 1, captures the essence of cyberspace as a three-dimensional network of computers with pure information moving between these computers, the definition itself is not inclusive enough because it does not specifically tell us the small details that make up cyberspace. Let us do that now by giving an expanded definition of cyberspace to include all components that make the resources of cyberspace. They include:

- hardware like computers, printers, scanners, servers and communication media;
- software that includes application and special programs, system backups and diagnostic programs, and system programs like operating systems and protocols;
- data in storage, transition, or undergoing modification;
- people that include users, system administrators, and hardware and software manufacturers;
- documentation which includes user information for hardware and software, administrative procedures, and policy documents; and
- supplies that include paper and printer cartridges.

These six components comprise the major divisions of cyberspace resources and together they form the cyberspace infrastructure and environment. Throughout this book, an attack on any one of these resources, therefore, will be considered as an attack on cyberspace resources.

Although all these resources make up cyberspace, and any one of them is a potential target for e-attacks, they do not have the same degree of vulnerability. Some are more vulnerable than others and, therefore, will be targeted more frequently by attackers.

Cyberspace has brought about an increasing reliance on these resources through computers running national infrastructures like telecommunications, electrical power systems, gas and oil storage and transportation, banking and finance, transportation, water supply systems, emergency services that include medical, police, fire, and rescue, and of course government services. These are central to national security, economic survival, and social well-being of people. Such infrastructures are deemed critical because their incapacitation could lead to chaos in any country.

A cyber threat is an intended or unintended illegal activity, an unavoidable or inadvertent event that has the potential or could lead to unpredictable, unintended, and adverse consequences on a cyberspace resource. A cyber attack or e-attack is a cyber threat that physically affects the integrity of any one of these cyberspace resources. Most cyber attacks can be put in one of three categories: natural or inadvertent attack; human error; or intentional threats [1].

Natural or inadvertent attack includes accidents originating from natural disasters like fire, floods, windstorms, lightning, and earthquakes. They usually occur very quickly without warning, and are beyond human capacity, often causing serious damage to affected cyberspace resources. There is not much that can be done to prevent natural disaster attacks on computer systems. However, precautions can be taken to lessen both the impact of such disasters and quicken the recovery from the damage they cause.

Human errors are caused by unintentional human actions. Unintended human actions are usually due to design problems. Such attacks are called *malfunctions*. Malfunctions, though occurring more frequently than natural disasters, are as unpredictable as natural disasters. They affect any cyber resource but they attack computer hardware and software resources more. In hardware, malfunctions can be a result of power failure or simply a power surge, electromagnetic influence, mechanical wear and tear, or human error. Software malfunctions result mainly from *logical errors* and occasionally from human errors during data entry. Malfunctions resulting from logical errors many times cause a system to halt. However, there are times when such errors may not cause a halt to the running program, but may be passed on to later stages of the computation. If that happens and the errors are not caught in time, they can result in bad decision making. A bad decision may cost an organization millions of dollars.

Most cyberspace attacks are intentional, originating from humans, caused by illegal or criminal acts from either insiders or outsiders. For the remainder of this chapter we are going to focus on intentional attacks.

Types of Attacks

Because of the many e-resources of cyberspace, the varying degrees of vulnerabilities of these resources, the motives of the attackers, and the many topographies involved, e-attacks fall into a number of types. We will put these types into two categories: penetration and denial of service attacks.

Penetration Attack

A penetration e-attack involves breaking into a system using known security vulnerabilities to gain access to any cyberspace resource. With full penetration, an intruder has full access to all that system's cyberspace resources or *e-resources*. Full penetration, therefore, allows an intruder to alter data files, change data, plant viruses, or install damaging Trojan horse programs into the system. It is also possible for intruders, especially if the victim computer is on a network, to use it as a launching pad to attack other network resources. According to Stallings [2], there are three classes of intruders.

(i)   Masquerader: This is a person who gains access to a computer system using other peoples' accounts without authorization.
(ii) Misfeasor: This is a legitimate user who gains access to system resources for which there is no authorization.
(iii) Clandestine user: This is a person with supervisory control who uses these privileges to evade or suppress auditing or access controls.

Penetration attacks can be local, where the intruder gains access to a computer on a LAN on which the program is run or global on a WAN like the Internet, where an e-attack can originate thousands of miles from the victim computer. This was the case in the "Love Bug" e-mail attack. For a long time, penetration attacks were limited to in-house employee generated attacks to systems and theft of company property. A limited form of system break-in from outsiders started appearing in the early 1970s when limited computer network communication became available. But as long as the technology was still in the hands of the privileged few, incidents of outsider system penetration were few. The first notable system penetration attack actually started in the mid–1980s with the San Francisco based 414-Club. The 414-Club was the first national news making hacker group. The group, based in the San Francisco area, named their group 414 after the Area Code of San Francisco they were in. They started a series of computer intrusion attacks via a Stanford University computer which they used to spread the attack across the country [3].

From that small but history making attack, other headline making attacks from Australia, Germany, Argentina and the United States followed. Ever since, we have been on a wild ride. There are three types of penetration attacks: viruses, non-virus malicious attacks from insiders, and non-virus malicious attacks from outsiders.

Viruses

Because viruses comprise a very big percentage of all cyberspace attacks, we will devote some time to them here. The term *virus* is derived from a Latin word *virus* which means poison. For generations, even before the birth of modern medicine, the term had remained mostly in medical circles, meaning a foreign agent injecting itself in a living body, feeding on it to grow and multiply. As it reproduces itself in the new environment, it spreads throughout the victim's body slowly disabling the body's natural resistance to foreign objects, weakening the body's ability to perform needed life functions and eventually causing serious, sometimes fatal, effects to the body.

A computer virus, defined as a self-propagating computer program designed to alter or destroy a computer system resource, follows almost the same pattern but instead of using the living body, it uses software to attach itself, grow, reproduce, and spread in the new environment. As it spreads in the new environment, it attacks major system resources that include the surrogate software itself, data, and sometimes hardware weakening the capacity of these resources to perform the needed functions and eventually bringing the system down.

The word virus was first assigned a non-biological meaning in the 1972 science fiction stories about the G.O.D. machine that were compiled in a book *When Harly Was One* by David Gerrod (Ballantine Books, First Edition, New York, NY, 1972). In the book, according to Karen Forcht, the term was first used to describe a piece of unwanted computer code [4]. Later association of the term with a real world computer program was by Fred Cohen, then a graduate student at the University of Southern California. Cohen wrote five programs, actually viruses, to run on a VAX 11/750 running UNIX, not to alter or destroy any computer resources but for class demonstration. During the demonstration, each virus obtained full control of the system within an hour [4].

Since this simple and rather harmless beginning, computer viruses have been on the rise. As both Table 3.1 and the graph in Figure 3.1 show, the growth of reported incidents of cyber attacks, most of which are virus attacks, has been explosive, almost exponential. In fact the growth of the Internet together with massive news coverage of virus incidents have caused an explosion of all types of computer viruses from sources scattered around the globe, with newer attacks at faster speeds than ever before. For more about the history and development of the computer virus the reader is referred to an extended discussion in Karen Forcht's book, *Computer Security Management* (Boyd & Fraser Publishing, 1994).

Number of Incidents Reported	
Year	Incidents
1988	6
1989	132
1990	252
1991	406
1992	773
1993	1,334
1994	2,340
1995	2,412
1996	2,573
1997	2,134
1998	3,734
1999	9,859
2000	21,756

Table 3.1 Number of Attack Incidents Reported to CERT (1988–2000)

Where do computer viruses come from? Just like human viruses, they are contracted when there is an encounter with a species that already has the virus. There are four main sources of viruses: movable computer disks like floppies, zips, and tapes; Internet downloadable software like beta software, shareware, and freeware; e-mail and e-mail attachments; and platform-free executable applets, like those Java language applets.

Although movable computer disks used to be the most common way of sourcing and transmitting viruses, new Internet technology has caused

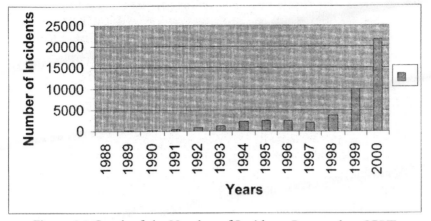

**Figure 3.1 Graph of the Number of Incidents Reported to CERT
(1988–2000)**
*(Source: Carnegie Mellon University, Software Engineering Institute,
http://www.cert.org/stats/cert_stats.html#incidents)*

this to decline. Viruses sourced from movable computer disks are either boot
viruses or disk viruses.

Boot viruses attack boot sectors on both hard and floppy disks. Disk
sectors are small areas on a disk that the hardware reads in single chunks.
For DOS formatted disks, sectors are commonly 512 bytes in length. Disk
sectors, although invisible to normal programs, are vital for the correct operation of computer systems because they form chunks of data the computer
uses. A boot sector is the first disk sector or first sector on a disk or diskette
that an operating system is aware of. It is called a boot sector because it contains an executable program the computer executes every time the computer
is powered up. Because of its central role in the operations of computer systems, the boot sector is very vulnerable to virus attacks and viruses use it as
a launching pad to attack other parts of the computer system. Viruses like
this sector because from it they can spread very fast from computer to computer, booting from that same disk. Boot viruses can also infect other disks
left in the disk drive of an infected computer.

Whenever viruses do not use the boot sector, they embed themselves,
as macros, in disk data or software. A macro is a small program embedded
in another program and executes when that program, the surrogate program,
executes. Macro viruses mostly infect data and document files like Microsoft
Word, templates, spreadsheets, and database files. All the following applications, for example, contain languages which allow the introduction of
macro viruses: Microsoft Word, Excel, Lotus 1-2-3, and Quattro Pro. Macro

viruses spread only within these specific environments, and the speed with which they spread depends on the frequency of use of infected documents in those applications. Examples of macro viruses are many including several varieties of both the *Concept* and *Nuclear*.

The advent of the Internet has made downloadable software the second most common source of viruses. Downloadable software include all downloadable types of software like freeware, shareware, and beta software. These types of software may have self-extracting viruses deliberately or accidentally implanted in them. Besides e-mail attachments, this is now the second fastest way to spread viruses. There are thousands of sites offering thousands of freeware, shareware, and beta software everyday. So if a virus is embedded into any one of these, it is likely to spread very far, wide, and fast.

Currently the most common sources of computer viruses are e-mail and e-mail attachments. This fact was demonstrated by the most recent newsmakers: "Melissa," the "Love Bug," and "Killer Resume." All three viruses were embedded in e-mail attachments. One reason e-mail and e-mail attachments are popular is because more than 50 percent of all Internet traffic is e-mails, so virus developers see it as the best vehicle for transmitting their deadly payloads.

The newest and perhaps the fastest-growing virus carrier is the Java applets. The Java Programming Language uses a Java applet to compile the source code on its Java machine and then migrate execution to a local browser. As web pages become more animated, applets are becoming more a medium of choice for virus transmission. There are some advantages to Java applets as virus conduits that still keep this method of spreading viruses low-keyed. Applets are more complicated and one may need more expertise to create a virus and embed it in an applet, other than one's own. And probably the most interesting advantage is that Java applets do not, as yet, have the capabilities to write to your machine's disk or memory; they simply execute in your browser. Until they acquire such capabilities, their ability to carry viruses will remain limited.

Let us now consider how viruses are transmitted. In order for a computer virus to infect the computer it must have a chance to be transmitted and deposited in a good location where it can execute its code. The transmission of these viruses has improved as computer technology improved. In those days when computers were stand-alone and computer networks were a preserve of the lucky few, computer viruses used to be transmitted by passing of infected floppy disks from one computer to another. The fully blown use of computer network communication, and the easy and almost universal access to the Internet have transformed and transcribed new methods of virus transmission. The proliferation of networking technologies, new developments in home personal Ethernet networks, and the miniaturization of personal computers have resulted in new and fast virus transmission and exchange techniques. This was no better demonstrated than in the recent successful transmission of the "Love Bug" e-mail virus when it circumvented the globe in a mere 12 hours.

When a fertile environment is found by the downloaded virus, it attaches itself to a surrogate software or a safe location where it will execute its code, modifying legitimate system resources so that its code is executed whenever these legitimate system resources are either opened or executed. Such resources may include the disk boot sector, which contains the code that is executed whenever the disk is used to boot the system, and other parts of the disk that contain software or data or other computer resources like memory. In non-boot sectors, the virus hides in software or data as macros which are executed whenever documents on the disk are opened with the relevant application.

The downloaded virus, depending on the type and motive, can either be immediately active or can lie dormant for a specified amount of time waiting for an event to activate it. An active virus hidden in a computer resource can copy itself straight away to other files or disks, thus increasing its chances of infection. The speed at which the virus spreads depends not only on the speed of the network and transmission media but also on how fast and long it can replicate unnoticed. Most viruses go undetected for long periods of time. In fact a lot of viruses manage to go undetected by either injecting themselves deep into legitimate code and disabling many of the codes' options that would cause it to be detected. When they succeeded in injecting themselves into a good hiding place, they may lie dormant for extended periods waiting for a trigger event to occur. The effects of a virus payload can range from harmless messages, data corruption and attrition to total destruction.

There are three ways viruses infect computer systems. The first of these is *boot sector penetration*. As we have seen in the previous section, a boot sector is usually the first sector on every disk. In a boot disk, the sector contains a chunk of code that powers up a computer as we have already discussed. In a non-bootable disk, the sector contains a File Allocation Table (FAT), which is automatically loaded first into computer memory to create a roadmap of the type and contents of the disk for the computer to access the disk. Viruses imbedded in this sector are assured of automatic loading into the computer memory. This is a very insidious way of system memory penetration by viruses.

A second method of infection is *macros penetration*. Since macros are small language programs that can only execute after imbedding themselves into surrogate programs, their penetration is quite effective. They are becoming popular because modern system application programs are developed in such a way that they can accept added user macros. The virus uses the added loophole to penetrate and utilize the built-in macro language specific to some popular product such as Microsoft Office

Parasites are a third method of infection. These are viruses that do not necessarily hide in the boot sector, nor use an incubator like the macros, but attach themselves to a healthy executable program and wait for any event where such a program is executed. These days, due to the spread of the Internet, this method of penetration is the most widely used and the most effective. Examples of parasite virus include Friday the 13th and Michelangelo viruses.

Once a computer attack is launched, most often a virus attack, the attacking agent scans the victim system looking for a healthy body for a surrogate. If it is found, the attacking agent tests to see if it has already been infected. Viruses do not like to infect themselves, hence, wasting their energy. If an uninfected body is found, then the virus attaches itself to it to grow, multiply, and wait for a trigger event to start its mission. The mission itself has three components:

- to look further for more healthy environments for faster growth, thus spreading more,
- to attach itself to any newly found body, and
- once embedded, either to stay in the active mode ready to go at any trigger event or to lie dormant until a specific event occurs.

Not only do viral sources and methods of infection differ; the viruses themselves are of several different types. In fact, one "type," called a *worm*, is actually not a virus at all, though the differences between a worm and a virus are few. They are both automated attacks, both self-generate or replicate new copies as they spread, and both can damage any resource they attack. The main difference between them, however, is that while viruses always hide in software as surrogates, worms are stand-alone programs. The origin of a worm is not very clear, but according to Peter Denning [3], the idea of a worm program that would invade computers and perform acts directed by the originator really started in 1975 in the science fiction novel *The Shockwave Rider* by John Brunner (Mass Market Paperback / Published 1990). However, the first real worm program was not written until early 1980 when John Shock and Jon Hupp working at Xerox Palo Alto Research Center wrote a program intended to replicate and locate idle workstations, on the network, for temporary use as servers [3]. Since then worms have been on the rise. The most outstanding worm programs include the Morris worm. Robert T. Morris, a computer science graduate student at Cornell University, created and released perhaps the first headline making worm program from an MIT computer. Instead of the program living on one infected computer, it created thousands of copies of itself on machines it infected. It is assumed to have infected approximately 6,000 computers, a great number in January 1990 [3].

A *memory resident* virus is more insidious, difficult to detect, fast spreading, and extremely difficult to eradicate. Once in memory, most viruses in this category simply disable a small part of or all of memory making it unavailable for the system to use. Because they attack the central storage part of a computer system, memory resident viruses are considered to do the most damage to the computer system. Once in memory, they attack any other program or data in the system. They are two types of memory resident viruses: *Transient*, the category that includes viruses that are only active when the inflicted program is executing, and *Resident*, a brand that attaches itself, via a surrogate software, to a portion of memory and remains active long after the surrogate program has finished executing. Examples of memory resident viruses include all boot sector viruses like the Israel virus [3].

Error generating viruses launch themselves most often in executable software. Once embedded, they attack the software to cause the software to generate errors. The errors can be either "hard" logical errors, resulting in a range of faults from simple momentary misses to complete termination of the software or they can be "soft" logical errors which may not be part of the software but just falsely generated errors causing the user to believe that the software has developed errors.

Data and program destroyers are viruses that attach themselves to a software and then use it as a conduit or surrogate for growth, replication, and as a launch pad for later attacks to this and other programs and data. Once attached to a software, they attack any data or program that the software may come in contact with, sometimes altering the contents, deleting, or completely destroying those contents. Some simply alter data and program files; others implant foreign codes in data and program files, yet others completely destroy all data and program files they come in contact with. If code is introduced in data files that are used by thousands of users or data is altered or removed from data files used by many, the effects can be severe. Familiar data and program destroying viruses are Friday the 13th and Michelangelo.

Most deadly of all are the viruses known as *system crushers*. Once introduced in a computer system, they completely disable the system. This can be done in a number of ways. One way is to destroy the system programs like operating system, compilers, loaders, linkers, and others. Another approach is to leave system software intact but the virus then replicates itself filling up system memory thus rendering the system useless.

In contrast, a *computer time theft virus* is not harmful in any way to system software and data. The goal of such a virus is to steal system time. The intruder has two approaches to this goal. One approach would be for the intruder to first stealthily become a legitimate user of the system and then later use all the system resources without any detection. Another way would be to prevent other legitimate users from using the system by first creating a number of system interruptions. This effectively puts other programs scheduled to run into indefinite wait queues. The intruder then gains the highest priority, like a superuser with full access to all system resources. With this approach, system intrusion is very difficult to detect.

While most viruses are known to alter or destroy data and programs, there are a few that literally attack and destroy system hardware. These are *hardware destroyers*, commonly known as *killer viruses*. Many of these viruses work by attaching themselves to micro-instructions, or "mic," like bios and device drivers. Once embedded into the mic, they may alter it in such ways that may cause the devices to move into positions that normally result in physical damage. For example, there are viruses that are known to lock up keyboards, disable mice, and cause disk read/write heads to move to non-existing sectors on the disk, thus causing the disk to crash.

Trojans are named after the famous Greek horse that concealed Greek soldiers as they tried to take over the city of Troy from the Phoenicians. The story has it that a huge hollow wooden horse full of Greek soldiers was left at the gates of the city of Troy as a "gift" from the Greeks to the people of Troy. Apparently the Greeks had tried to take the city of Troy several times and failed each time. The horse was taken inside the city walls by the people of Troy and when night befell the city, Greek soldiers, under cover of darkness, emerged from the horse's belly, opened the city gates for the remainder of the Greek soldiers, and destroyed the city. From this legend, anything that abuses trust from within an entity is referred to as a Trojan horse. Trojan horse viruses use the same tricks the legendary Greeks used. They hide inside trusted common programs like compilers, editors, and other commonly used programs.

Logic or time bombs are viruses that penetrate the system, embedding themselves in the system's software, using it as a conduit and waiting to attack once a trigger goes off. Trigger events can vary in type depending on the motive of the virus. Most triggers are timed events. There are various types of these viruses including Columbus Day, Valentine's Day, Jerusalem-D, and the Michelangelo which was meant to activate on Michelangelo's

517th birthday anniversary. The most recent time bomb is the "Y2K bug," which had millions of people scared as the year 2000 rolled in. The bomb was an unintentional design flaw of a date where the year field did not use four digits. The scare was just a scare; very few effects were noted.

Trapdoor viruses find their way into the system through parts of the system and application software weak points. A trapdoor is a special set of instructions that allow a user to bypass normal security precautions to enter a system. Quite often software manufacturers, during software development and testing, intentionally leave trapdoors in their products, usually undocumented, as secret entry points into the programs so that modification can be done on the programs at a later date. Trapdoors are also used by programmers as testing points. As always the case, trapdoors can also be exploited by malicious people including programmers themselves. In a trapdoor attack, an intruder may deposit a virus-infected data file on a system instead of actually removing, copying, or destroying the existing data files. There is an interesting science trapdoor scenario in the 1983 film *War Games*, where a trapdoor was successfully used by a hacker to gain access to a military installation in the Cheyenne Mountains in the state of Utah. The hacker who was penetrating a military computer which was programmed to react to nuclear attack threat was accidentally caught off guard. When the computer detected the intrusion, it mistook it to be a nuclear threat. According to the movie script, the computer automatically went into the loaded pre-launch activities for launching a nuclear missile. The only way it could be stopped, which the original programmer who created the program successfully tried, was through a trapdoor. However, without a password, he and the intruder could not stop the launch program. At the end of the movie, as expected, the hacker manages to crack the military password file and saves humanity.

Some viruses are *jokes* or *hoaxes* that do not destroy or interfere with the working of the computer system. They are meant to be a simple nuisance to the user. Many of these types of viruses are sent to one or more users for no other reasons than the sender having fun. Jokes and or hoax viruses are for that purpose alone. Hoaxes usually are meant to create scare while jokes are meant to create fun for the recipients. However, fun may not always be the result. Sometimes what was meant to be a joke or a hoax virus may end up creating mayhem.

We can follow Stepheson's [6] virus classification and put all these viruses into the following categories:

(i) Parasites: These are viruses that attach themselves to executable files and replicate to attack other files whenever the victims' programs are executed.

(ii)   Boot sector: These were seen earlier. They are viruses that affect the boot sector of a disk.

(iii) Stealth: These are viruses that are designed to hide themselves against any anti-virus software.

(iv)   Memory-resident: As seen earlier, there are viruses that use system memory as a beachhead to attack other programs.

(v)   Polymorphic: These are viruses that mutate at every infection making their detection difficult.

Theft of Proprietary Information

Theft of proprietary information involves the acquisition and copying or distribution of that proprietary information to the third party. This may also involve certain types of knowledge obtained through legitimate employment. It also includes all information as defined in the intellectual property statutes such as copyrights, patents, trade secrets, and trademarks. These types of attacks originate mainly from insiders within the employee ranks who may steal the information for a number of motives. As we stated in Chapter 2, companies are reluctant to report these types of attacks for fear of bad publicity and public disclosure of their trade secrets.

Fraud

The growth of online services and access to the Internet have provided fertile ground for cyberspace fraud or *cyberfraud*. New novel online consumer services that include cybershopping, online banking, and other online "conveniences" have enabled consumers to do business online. However, crooks and intruders have also recognized the potential of cyberspace with its associated new technologies. These technologies are creating new and better ways to commit crimes against unsuspecting consumers.

Most online computer attacks motivated by fraud are in a form that will give the intruder consumer information like social security numbers, credit information, medical records, and a whole host of individual vital information usually stored on computer system databases.

Sabotage

Sabotage is a process of withdrawing efficiency. It may also mean either to slacken up and interfere with the quantity or effects to one's skills which may eventually lead to low quality and quantity of service expected of that individual. Sabotage as a system attack is an internal process which can be initiated by either an insider or an outsider. Sabotage motives vary depending on the attacker but most are meant to strike the target, most times employers, for the attacker's benefit. The widespread use of the Internet has greatly increased the potential for and incidents of these types of attacks.

Espionage

By the end of the Cold War, the United States, as a leading military, economic, and information superpower, found itself a constant target of military espionage. As the Cold War faded, military espionage shifted and gave way to economic espionage. In its pure form, economic espionage targets economic trade secrets which, according to the 1996 U.S. Economic Espionage Act, are defined as all forms and types of financial, business, scientific, technical, economic, or engineering information and all types of intellectual property including patterns, plans, compilations, program devices, formulas, designs, prototypes, methods, techniques, processes, procedures, programs, and or codes, whether tangible or not, stored or not, compiled or not [7]. To enforce this Act and prevent computer attacks targeting American commercial interests, the American federal law authorizes law enforcement agencies to use wiretaps and other surveillance means to curb computer supported information espionage.

Network and Vulnerability Scanning

Scanners are programs that keep a constant electronic surveillance of a computer or a network looking for computers and network devices with vulnerabilities. Computer vulnerabilities may be in the system hardware or software. Scanning the network computers for vulnerabilities allows the attacker to determine all possible weaknesses and loopholes in the system. This opens up possible attack avenues.

Password Crackers

Password crackers are actually worm algorithms. According to Don Seely, these algorithms have four parts: the first part, which is the most important, gathers password data used by the remaining three parts from hosts and user accounts [8]. Using this information, it then tries to either generate individual passwords or to crack passwords it comes across. During the cracking phase, the worm saves the name, the encrypted password, the directory, and the user information field for each account.

The second and third parts trivially break passwords that can be easily broken using information already contained in the passwords. This is based on the fact that around 30 percent of all passwords can be guessed using only literal variations or comparison with favorite passwords [9]. This list of favorite passwords consists of roughly 432 words, most of them proper nouns and common English words [9]. And the last part takes words in the user dictionaries and tries to decrypt them one by one. This may prove to be very time consuming and also a little harder. But with time it may yield good guesses.

Employee Network Abuse

Although on the surface and traditionally concerns of computer attacks on companies and corporations have been focused on outside penetration of systems, inside attacks have chronically been presenting serious problems in the workplace. An insider is someone who has been explicitly or implicitly granted access privileges that allow him or her the use of a particular system's facilities. Recent incidents, including the Bank of New York's Russian money laundering fiasco, have spotlighted the fundamental problems associated with insider system misuse. Insider net abuse attacks are fundamentally driven by financial fraud, vendettas, and other forms of the intentional misuse. Nearly all insider net abuses are covered up.

A number of things have kept this rather serious problem off the radar including [10]:

(i)   the fact that system security technology does not as yet distinguish inside system attacks and those originating from outside;

(ii)   lack of system authentication that would prevent insiders from masquerading as someone else;

(iii) unchecked top management's all-powerful root privileges;

(iv) employees' assumption that once given access privileges they can roam the entire system;

(v)   local systems' audit trails that are inadequate or compromised; and

(vi) lack of definitive policy on what constitutes insider net abuse in any given application.

Embezzlement

Embezzlement is an inside job by employees. It happens when a trusted employee fraudulently appropriates company property for personal gains. Embezzlement is widespread and happens every day to both large and small businesses, though small businesses are less likely to take the precautions necessary to prevent it. Online embezzlement is even more challenging because it may never be found. And if found sometimes it takes very long to correct thereby causing more damage.

Computer Hardware Parts Theft

Computer hardware components are increasingly becoming a target of information thieves. This type of e-attack is currently highlighted by the theft of laptops. According to Wally Bock, laptops are becoming such a popular target for thieves that Computer World added $150 to the cost of every machine they sell probably for insurance. In 1997, the Safeware Insurance Company handled a billion dollars worth of claims for stolen laptops. That's a jump of 28 percent from 1996. In turn, 1996 was a 27 percent jump from 1995 [11].

Laptop attacks recently received prominence because of the four highly publicized episodes of computer hardware parts theft. The first three involved the theft of laptop computers from relatively secure environments. On two occasions, the U.S. Department of Defense has lost laptops from the offices of the Pentagon. The other laptop theft occurred at the British Ministry of Defense although this was categorically denied by the British government.

In the latest episode of the computer hardware component theft saga, two little disks mysteriously disappeared from the U.S.'s Los Alamos National Weapons Laboratories. The two small disks, about the size of a deck of cards, were said to contain highly technical information that would be used by a nuclear emergency response team to locate and dismantle a nuclear device from nuclear-able countries like the United States, Russia, China, France, and others in that exclusive club. A nuclear emergency is an actual nuclear attack, a nuclear accident, or a terrorist nuclear attack. The comedy and circus-like environment that surrounded the disappearance and mysterious reappearance of the little disks has created interest in what would have been a routine theft. The drives, believed to have been stolen about six months earlier, were last reported seen on April 7, 2000. In circumstances that seem like they were taken from a spy novel, the two drives reappeared in June 2000 in a secure area, previously searched behind a copier. The fact that the area had been previously searched, raised more questions like when the disks were actually returned, whether the disks were copied, how long they had been missing, and who did it?

While this episode and the three earlier episodes of the computer hardware components' theft were highly publicized, there are hundreds of similar cases with probably more value that are never reported.

Denial of Service Attacks

Denial of service attacks, commonly known as distributed denial of service (DDoS) attacks, are not penetration attacks. They do not change, alter, destroy, or modify system resources. They, however, affect the system through diminishing the system's ability to function; hence, they are capable of bringing a system down without destroying its resources. These types of attacks made headlines when the Canadian teen attacked Internet heavyweights Amazon, eBay, E*Trade, and news leader CNN. DDoS attacks have been on the rise. Like penetration e-attacks, DDoS attacks can also be either local, where they can shut down LAN computers, or global, originating thousands of miles away on the Internet, as was the case in the Canadian generated DDoS attacks.

Most of the attacks in this category have already been discussed in Chapter 2. They include among others IP-spoofing, SYN flooding, smurfing, buffer overflow, and sequence number sniffing.

Motives of E-Attacks

Although hacking has still a long way to go before it can become a respectable pastime, to those doing it it can be a full-time "job" or hobby, taking countless hours per week to learn the tricks of the trade, developing, experimenting, and executing the art of penetrating multi-user computers' systems. Why do hackers spend such a good portion of their time hacking? Is it scientific curiosity, mental stimulation, greed, or personal attention? It is difficult to exclusively answer this question because the true roots of hacker motives run much deeper than that. Let us look at a few:

Some attacks are likely the result of personal vendettas. There are many causes that lead to vendettas. The demonstrations at the last World Trade Organization (WTO) in Seattle, Washington, subsequent demonstrations at the meetings in Washington, D.C., of both the World Bank and the International Monetary Fund and the G8 meeting in Genoa, Italy, are indicative of the growing discontent of the masses; masses unhappy with big business, multi-nationals, globalization, and a million others. This discontent is driving a new breed of wild, rebellious, young people to hit back at systems that they see as not solving world problems and benefitting all of mankind. These mass computer attacks are increasingly being used as paybacks for what the attacker or attackers consider to be injustices done that need to be avenged. However, most vendetta attacks are for mundane reasons as a promotion denied, a boyfriend or girlfriend taken, an ex-spouse given child custody, and other situations that may involve family and intimacy issues.

Some attacks at least begin as jokes, hoaxes, or pranks. Hoaxes are warnings that are actually scare alerts started by one or more malicious people and are passed on by innocent users who think that they are helping the community by spreading the warning. Most hoaxes are viruses although there are hoaxes that are computer related folklore stories and urban legends or true stories. Virus hoaxes are most times false reports about non-existent viruses that cause panic, especially to the majority of users who do not know how viruses work. Some hoaxes can get extremely widespread as they are mistakenly distributed by individuals and companies with the best of intentions. Although many virus hoaxes are false scares, there are some which may have some truth about them, but which often become greatly exaggerated such as "The Good Times" and "The Great Salmon." Virus hoaxes infect mailing lists, bulletin boards, and Usenet newsgroups. Worried system administrators sometimes contribute to this scare by posting dire warnings to their employees which become hoaxes themselves.

Some attacks are motivated by "hacker's ethics" — a collection of motives that make up the hacker character. Steven Levy lists these as follows [12]:

- Access to computers — and anything which might teach you something about the way the world works — should be unlimited and total. Always yield to the Hands-On imperative!
- All information should be free.
- Mistrust authority — promote decentralization.
- Hackers should be judged by their hacking, not bogus criteria such as degrees, age, race, or position.
- You can create art and beauty on a computer.
- Computers can change your life for the better.

If any of these beliefs is violated, a hacker will have a motive.

Terrorism: Our increasing dependence on computers and computer communication has opened up a can of worms we now know as electronic terrorism. Electronic terrorism — that is, hitting individuals by hitting the banking and the military systems — is by a new breed of hacker, who no longer holds the view of cracking systems as an intellectual exercise but as a way of gaining from the action. The "new" hacker is a cracker who knows and is aware of the value of information that he/she is trying to obtain or compromise. But cyber-terrorism is not only about obtaining information, it is also about instilling fear and doubt and compromising the integrity of the data.

Political and military espionage is another motive. For generations countries have been competing for supremacy of one form or another. During the Cold War, countries competed for military spheres. At the end of the Cold War, the espionage turf changed from military to gaining access to highly classified commercial information that would not only let them know what other countries are doing but also might give them either a military or commercial advantage without spending a lot of money on the effort. It is not surprising, therefore, that the spread of the Internet has given a boost and a new lease on life to a dying Cold-War profession. Our high dependency on computers in the national military and commercial establishments has given espionage a new fertile ground. Electronic espionage has a lot of advantages over its old-fashioned, trench-coated, sun-glassed, and gloved Hitchcock-style cousin. For example, it is far cheaper to implement, it can gain access into places which would be inaccessible to human spies, and it saves embarrassments in case of failed or botched attempts, and it can be carried out at a place and time of choice. One of the first electronic espionage incidents that involved massive computer networks was by Marcus H., the West German hacker, who in 1986 along with accomplices attacked military, universities, and research organization centers in the United States. Over a period of 10 months, he attacked over 450 computers and successfully penetrated over 40 that started with the Lawrence Berkeley Laboratory, through which he attacked U.S. Army Bases in Japan, Germany, Washington, D.C., and Alabama; U.S. Naval Bases in Panama City, Naval Shipyard and Data Center in Norfolk, Virginia; U.S. Air Force Bases in Germany and El Segudo, California; defense contractors in Richardson, Texas, Redondo Beach, California; and universities that included the University of Boston, a university in Atlanta, Georgia, the University of Pittsburgh, Pennsylvania, the University of Rochester, New York, the University of Pasadena, California, and the University of Ontario, Canada. His list also had national research laboratories including Livermore, the National Computing Center in Livermore, and research laboratories in Pasadena, California. As the list demonstrates, his main motive, according to Clifford Stoll, was computers operated by the military and by defense contractors, research organizations, and research universities [13]. Marcus and his accomplices were passing the information they were getting on to the KGB in the then–USSR. Marcus was arrested and convicted, together with his accomplices, Dirk B. and Peter C. [13].

Another type of espionage that may motivate a cyber attack is business (competition) espionage. As businesses become global and world markets become one global bazaar, business competition for ideas and market strategies is becoming very intense. According to Jonathan Calof, professor of management at the University of Ottawa, sought information for business competitiveness comes from primary sources, most of all the employees [14].

Because of this, business espionage is mainly targeting people, more specifically employees. Company employees, and especially those working in company computer systems, are targeted the most. Cyber sleuthing and corporate computer attacks are the most used business espionage technique that usually involves physical system penetration for trophies like company policy, management and marketing data. It may also involve sniffing, electronic surveillance of company executive electronic communications, and company employee chat rooms for information.

Some cyber attacks spring from a very old motivation: hatred. Hate as a motive of attack originates from an individual or individuals with a serious dislike of another person or group of persons based on a string of human attributes that may include national origin, gender, race, or mundane ones like the manner of speech one uses. The attackers then incensed by one or all of these attributes contemplate and carry out attacks of vengeance often rooted in ignorance.

Some attacks may be motivated by a desire for personal gain. Such motives spring from the selfishness of individuals who are never satisfied with what they have and are always wanting more, mostly financial. It is this need to get more that drives the attacker to plan and execute an attack.

Finally, cyber attack sometimes occurs as a result of ignorance. Unintended acts may lead to destruction of information and other systems resources. Such acts usually occur as a result of individuals (authorized or not, but in either case ignorant of the workings of the system) stumbling upon weaknesses or performing a forbidden act that results in system resource modification or destruction.

Topography of Attacks

E-attackers must always use specific patterns in order to reach their victims. When targeting one individual, they use a pattern of attack different from one they would use if their target was a group of green people. In this case they would use a different pattern that would only reach and affect green people. However, if they wanted to affect every one regardless, they would use still a different pattern. The pattern chosen, therefore, is primarily based on the type of victim(s), motive, location, method of delivery, and a few other things. There topographics are four of these patterns and we will call them topographies. These are illustrated in figures 3.2, 3.3, 3.4 and 3.5, respectively.

One-to-One

These e-attacks originate from one attacker and are targeted to a known victim. They are personalized attacks where the attacker knows the victim and sometimes the victim may know the attacker. One-to-one attacks are usually motivated by hate, personal vendettas, a desire for personal gain, or an attempt to make a joke, though business espionage may also be involved.

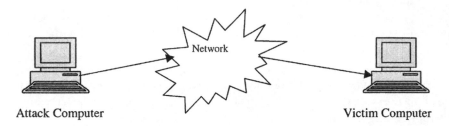

Attack Computer   Victim Computer

Figure 3.2 One-to-One Topography

One-to-Many

These attacks are fueled by anonymity. In most cases the attacker does not know any of the victims. And in all cases, the attacker will, at least that is what they assume, remain anonymous to the victims. This topography has been the technique of choice in the last two to three years because it is one of the easiest to carry out. The motives that drive attackers to use this technique are hate, a desire for personal satisfaction, or an attempt to play a joke or to intimidate people with a hoax.

Many-to-One

These attacks so far have been rare, but they have recently picked up momentum as the distributed denial of services attacks have once again gained favor in the hacker community. In a many-to-one attack technique, the attacker starts the attack by using one host to spoof other hosts, the secondary victims, which are then used as the new source of an avalanche of attacks on a selected victim. These types of attacks need a high degree of coordination and, therefore, may require advanced planning and a good understanding of the infrastructure of the network. They also require a very well executed selection process in choosing the secondary victims and then eventually the final victim. Attacks in this category are driven by personal vendetta, hate, terrorism, or a desire for attention and fame.

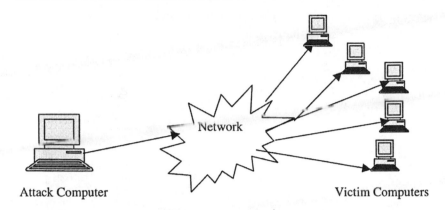

Figure 3.3 One-to-Many Topography

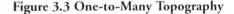

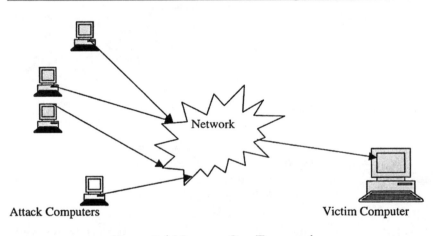

Figure 3.4 Many-to-One Topography

Many-to-Many

As in the previous topography, attacks using this topography are rare; however, there has been an increase recently in reported attacks using this technique. For example, in some of the recent DDoS cases, there have been a select group of sites chosen by the attackers as secondary victims. These are then used to bombard another select group of victims. The numbers involved in each group may vary from a few to several thousands. As was the case in the previous many-to-one topography, attackers using this technique need a good understanding of the network infrastructure and a good and precise selection process to pick the secondary victims and eventually selecting the final pool of victims. Attacks utilizing this topology are mostly driven by a number of motives including terrorism, a desire for attention and fame, or a desire to pull off a joke or hoax.

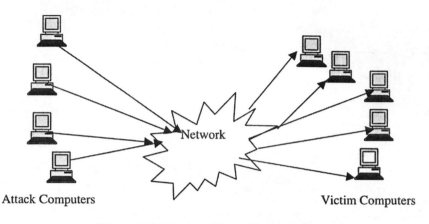

Attack Computers   Victim Computers

Figure 3.5 Many-to-Many Topography

How Hackers Plan E-Attacks

Few computer attacks are developed and delivered in a few hours. The processes are always well drawn. There is always a motive followed by a plan. It is these carefully well planned origination, development, and incubation periods of an attack that lead to successful execution of e-attacks. If only the law enforcement agencies and society as a whole were to use these planning periods as windows of opportunity to snoop into these activities before they hatch, computer crimes would be significantly reduced. But unfortunately this may never happen because of the elaborate and varying sequences of steps leading to attacks. Studies of hacker activities from interviews and court papers have shown that an actual attack has the following sequence of steps.

- There is always a motive that must precede all other activities before the attack.
- Targets are always identified based on the motive(s).
- Programs are developed. Several programs may be needed, some to scan for network and system vulnerabilities and others to deliver the attacker payload.
- Once the targets are identified and the programs written, then,

depending on the topography of attack, scanners are downloaded to search for network weak points and devices and develop a full picture of the victim and LAN configuration. Operating systems and applications running on the victim site are also identified and platform and network vulnerability noted.

- Using information from the scan, the first attempts are made from a list of selected target victims. The techniques used in the initial attack depend on whether the planned attack is going to be a distributed denial of service or a penetration. In most penetration attacks, the initial attempt may include simple attacks like using FTP, telnet, remote login, and password-guessing. Once the initial penetration is successful, then known system security loopholes as revealed by the scanners are attempted. These attempts may lead to the intruder gaining even higher security and access privileges that can put the intruder in full control before the full blown attack can commerce.

- Once the initial attempts are successful, they are then used as a beachhead into launching a full-scale attack on the selected targets.

Most Common Computer Security Flaws

According to the SANS Institute, a cooperative of computer security experts, the most common computer security flaws as reported for (1999) are as follows [15]:

BIND Weaknesses

This involves the binding of a system name to the numeric IP address making it easy to locate systems on the Internet by name without having to know specific IP addresses. This binding has security weaknesses that can be exploited by an intruder. Since the Berkeley Internet Name Domain package is the most widely used implementation of Domain Name Service (DNS), it is a favorite target for attack.

Vulnerable CGI

Common Gateway Interface programs and application extensions installed on web servers provide interactivity between web pages. Many web servers come with sample CGI programs installed by default. If it is not reprogrammed or changed by the system manager or security chief, the sample CGI can be penetrated by intruders who know it, and hence system security compromised.

Remote Procedure Call (RPC) Weaknesses

The RPC's feature allows programs on one computer to execute remote programs on a second computer. This feature is widely used in a number of distributed systems and most network services such as shared files. This weakness allows the intruder immediate root access on the remote system and, therefore, remote system security compromises.

RDS Security Hole: Many Internet-based applications have several needs to address including being able to service a large number of users and to operate independently as if they were running on stand-alone computers. To achieve these objectives, an Internet server needs to handle its resources as efficiently as possible. Microsoft's Internet Information Server (IIS) contains a Remote Data Services (RDS) to do this. But this Microsoft's RDS, widely used on Microsoft Windows NT and Windows 2000 web server software, contains many programming flaws. These flaws in IIS' RDS are then exploited by malicious users to run remote commands with administrator privileges.

Sendmail Buffer Overflow

Sendmail is a program that uses the Simple Mail Transfer Protocol (SMTP) over a computer network to send and receive e-mail messages. It sends a message doing internetworking, as necessary, to one or more recipients. For most e-mails using either UNIX or Linux, an intruder can overflow buffers in both setuid UNIX and setuid Linux programs, giving the intruder a root shell, thus allowing the intruder immediate root access. The widespread use of Sendmail on the Internet makes it a prime target of attackers.

Sadmind and Mountd

Sadmind is a daemon used by Solstice AdminSuite applications to perform distributed system administration operations such as adding users. It runs as a root in Solaris computer systems thus allowing any code launched to run with root privileges, resulting, therefore, in a root compromise. Mountd, a super-user-run daemon, is both a Remote Procedure Call (RPC) and Network File System (NFS) mount request server that answers file system mount requests. Before answering to the requests, it first determines which file systems are available for mounting and by which machines and what file systems they are mounted and by which clients. This information is then used to control and arbitrate access to Network File System (NFS) mounts on UNIX hosts. Buffer overflows in these two applications can very easily be exploited by intruders allowing them root access.

File and Information Sharing

Uncontrolled and improperly configured sharing of files and information over networks can expose critical system files or give full-file system access that may lead to intrusion into the network. Global file sharing and inappropriate information sharing via NFS and Windows 2000 ports 135–445, Windows NT ports 135–139 or UNIX NFS exports on port 2049 are examples that can lead to network intrusion [16].

User Passwords

Although passwords seem to be the first and easiest defense to system intrusion, they are one of the weakest system penetration points. This is made possible through uncontrolled or lavishly distributed passwords, no passwords, or weak passwords to root/administrators, systems with "demo" or "guest" accounts with no passwords, systems with widely known default passwords, no passwords for service workers, and administration accounts with default passwords. Other password faults include system passwords that are easily guessable and blank passwords.

IMAP and POP Buffer Overflow

The Internet Message Access Protocol (IMAP) is a method of accessing electronic mail and bulletin board messages from a mail server. It performs these services by allowing a "client" e-mail program to access remote server messages as if they were local. The Post Office Protocol (POP) works in the same way as IMAP except it works best with only a single computer involved in the transfer. Both IMAP and POP are widely used remote access mail protocols allowing users to access their e-mail accounts across networks. If any one of these protocols is vulnerable, remote intruders can, through these vulnerable IMAP and POP servers, gain root access.

Default SNMP Community Strings

Simple Network Management Protocol (SNMP) is a network management protocol developed in 1988 to solve communication problems between different types of networks. Since then, it has become a de facto standard. It works by exchanging network information through the five protocol data units (PDUs). This protocol suite manages information obtained from network entities such as hosts, routers, switches, hubs, and so on. The information collected from these various network entities via SNMP variable queries is sent to a management station. Also information events, called traps, notifying of critical changes such as changes to interface status, and packet collisions can be sent from entities to these management stations. These domains of SNMP management stations and entities are grouped together in "communities." These communities, commonly known as *community strings*, are used as an authentication method in information retrieval/traps. Two types of community strings are in common use: read, which is default public, and write, which is default private. A read community has privileges to retrieve variables from SNMP entities and a write community has privileges to read as well as write to entity variables. SNMP employs these units to monitor and administer all types of network-connected devices, data transmissions, and network events such as terminal start-ups or shut-downs. However, these SNMP entities are unencrypted. It is possible for any intruder to have full administrator access to these SNMP facilities which has the potential for abuse of privileges that include the ability to modify host name, network interface state, IP forwarding and routing, state of network sockets (including the ability to terminate active TCP sessions and listening sockets) and the ARP cache. An attacker also has full read access to all SNMP facilities [17].

Some Statistics Regarding Attacks

Table 3.2 shows the most popular attacks on the Internet based on National Institute of Standards and Technology's May 1999 *Bulletin* [16]. Table 3.3 shows the most popular motives based on sources [18].

Table 3.4 and 3.5 show the top ten most reported viruses for 1998 and 1999 respectively, according to Sophas Plc, a data security company that produces software and hardware for data encryption, authentication and secure erasure [19].

Attack
Sendmail
ICQ
Smurf
Teardrop
IMAP
Back Orifice
Netbus
WinNuke
Nmap

Table 3.2 Most Popular Attacks (1999)

Number	Motive	Foreign	Domestic Outsider	Domestic Insider
1	Espionage	√	√	√
2	Greed	√	√	√
3	Terrorism	√	√	√
4	Thrill/fun	√	√	√
5	Vendetta		√	√
6	Malice		√	√
7	Hate	√	√	√
8	Attention	√	√	√
9	Warfare	√	√	
10	Embezzlement			√
11	Net abuse	√	√	√
12	Password crack	√	√	√
13	Information Theft	√	√	√
14	Virus	√	√	√
15	DDoS	√	√	
16	Sabotage	√	√	√
17	Scanning	√	√	√

Table 3.3 Popular Motives Based on Sources

Virus Name	Percentage of reporting (%)
XM/Laroux	16
W95/CIH-10xx	10
WM/CAP	10
WM97/Class	6
Form	6
CMOS4	5
Anticmos	4
WM/Concept	4
WM/CopyCap	3
Parity Boot	2

Table 3.4 Most Commonly Reported Viruses in 1998

Virus Name	Percentage of Reporting (%)
XM/Laroux	16.7
WM97/Ethan	10.4
WM97/Marker	9.9
WM97/Class	8.2
W32/Ska-Happy99	7.8
WM97/Footer	7.0
WM97/Melissa	5.7
W95/CIH-10xx	5.4
Form	2.5
W32/ExploreZip	1.7

Table 3.5 Most Commonly Reported Viruses in 1999

Conclusion

The computer revolution that gave birth to the Internet, and hence to cyberspace, has in most ways changed human life for the better. The benefits of the revolution far outweigh the problems we have so far discussed in this and proceeding chapters. People have benefited far more from the revolution in every aspect of life than they have been affected negatively. And it is expected, from almost all signs, that new developments in computer technology and new research will yield yet better benefits for humanity.

However, while this is the case, we should not ignore the inconveniences, at least up to now, of the social and ethical upheavals that are perpetuated by the technology. We need to find ways to prevent future computer attacks, if not to eliminate them. Our focus, as we work on the root causes of these attacks, is to understand what they are, who generates them, and why. Dealing with these questions and finding answers to them is not an easy task for a number of reasons. Among those reasons are the following:

- The nature, topography, and motives of e-attacks change as computer technology changes.
- Since 80 to 90 percent of all e-attacks are virus-based, the development of computer viruses is getting better and faster because of new developments in computer programming. If current trends continue, the cut-and-paste programming we are using today will get even better resulting in better viruses, virus macros, and applets.
- Current development in genetic programming, artificial intelligence, and web-based script development all point to new and faster developments of viruses and other programming-based types of e-attacks.
- The development in network programming, network infrastructure, and programming languages with large API libraries will continue to contribute to a kind of a "team" effort in virus development where virus wares and scripts are easily shared and passed around.
- Free-downloadable header tools are widely available. There are thousands of hacker tools and wares on hundreds of hacker web sites that will eventually make the designs of viruses a thrilling experience.
- The public is still impressed by the "intelligence" of hackers.

For these and other reasons we have not touched on, e-attacks are likely to continue, and the public, through legislation, enforcement, self-regulation, and education, must do whatever possible to keep cyberspace civilized.

Chapter 4

Cyber Crimes: Costs and Social Consequences

In 1997 the U.S. National Security Agency, using 35 hired hackers, launched a simulated attack codenamed "Eligible Receiver" on the U.S. electronic infrastructure that included the Department of Energy (DOE), the Department of Defense (DOD), power grids, parts of 911 communication centers in several U.S. cities including Washington, D.C., and a selected number of U.S. Navy Crusher systems [1]. The purpose of "Eligible Receiver" was to determine the degree of U.S. preparedness for an electronic Pearl Harbor.

The exercise was a result of long, sometimes partisan discussions about the U.S. preparedness for a national electronic attack. At that time, there was a serious lack of data collection and analysis by U.S. intelligence agencies, business, and financial communities that would have provided lead information, assessment, and preparedness of the nation for an electronic attack on the national information infrastructure. The 1996 Brown Commission Report on the Role and Capabilities of the U.S. Intelligence Community that would have been the most appropriate study of the threat, did not address the issue beyond only stating that "collecting information about information warfare threats posed by other nations or by non-governmental groups to U.S. systems is, however, a legitimate mission of the intelligence community." But the report acknowledged that this mission would become important and, therefore, requires better definition [2]. In fact in the 1996 Congressional Hearings on "Intelligence and Security in Cyberspace," a senior member of the intelligence community in charge of collecting such data compared the efforts in place at the time to a "toddler soccer game where everyone just runs around trying to kick the ball somewhere" [2].

This is not a problem limited to the United States only; country after country around the globe are facing similar problems. Very few countries, if any, have assessed and analyzed any information on their information infrastructure, on how an electronic attack can not only affect their national security, but also other essential infrastructures like businesses, power grids, financial and public institutions affected by this lack of preparedness. There are various reasons to this lack of information including the following:

- In nearly all countries there is no required reporting mechanism in government agencies, even the private sector, to detect intrusions and report such intrusions.
- In the private sector, there is very little interest in reporting of any system related intrusions. This is a result of the fear of marketplace forces that would expose management's weaknesses to the shareholder community and competitors.
- There is no adequate enforcement of existing reporting mechanisms. In the United States, for example, there are legal requirements on the book that would require both public and private sectors to report system intrusions. Under these requirements banks must report disappearance in unexplained shortages of funds over $5000 or more [1]. In addition the Federal Security and Exchange Commission (SEC) requires all financial institutions that include securities firms and publicly traded corporations to report certain activities.
- The insider effect. There are various reports all pointing to a blank picture about the effect of insider intruders to the overall detection and reporting of e-attacks. It is reported in some studies that a majority of all e-attacks are generated and started by inside employees. This makes the job of detection and reporting very murky. It is like having an arsonist working in the fire department.
- Many nations have no required and trained security agencies to fight e-attacks.

Because of and probably as a result of all these, individuals, businesses, and nations are living with the threat of a cyber atomic bomb that may come any day, anytime, and from anywhere. As computer proliferation around the globe grows, this threat increases, and there is every reason to be concerned. While "Eligible Receiver" was a mock exercise, there have been thousands of real ones, the majority of which go undetected and fewer yet are reported. To illustrate the potential danger of cyber attacks and the devastation and loss they can cause, let us look at the list of a few of those that somehow got into the news [1].

In 1995, when little thought was given to computer systems intrusions, 21-year-old Julio Cesar Ardita, in Buenos Aires, Argentina, illegally broke into computer systems of several U.S. universities including Harvard, Cal Tech, the University of Massachusetts, and Northwestern University. He also broke into the Department of Defense and NASA computer systems. It is also believed that the same person broke into systems in other countries including Brazil, Chile, Korea, Mexico, and Taiwan. The information Ardita obtained from these systems was not benign; it included excessive information on government satellites and radiation energy [5].

In 1996 the Pentagon detected more than 25,000 break-in attempts according to the U.S. General Accounting Office. What is even more surprising is that 65 percent of these were successful. This, seen in light of the fact that the Pentagon conducts 95 percent of its communication over commercial communication networks, is worrisome [6].

In a series of coordinated intrusions over a period of two years, 1997 and 1998, an 18-year-old Israeli boy named Enud Tenebum, with his 16-year-old California companion, broke into 11 Navy and Air Force unclassified systems. The Pentagon went on 24-hour shifts, as they tried to identify the sources and individuals behind the intrusions. After several weeks of investigations, the culprits were apprehended. But by the Pentagon's own admission, "the kids were able to create an awful lot of disruptions in the Department of Defense (DoD)" [15]. Although the attack did not compromise any serious classified information, it, however, because of its breadth and timing (it occurred when the United States was preparing to attack Iraq), highlighted the vulnerability of the DoD and it was a wake-up call to the Pentagon and U.S. administration to speed up efforts to combat similar incursions.

According to the FedCIRC (Federal Computer Incident Response Center), the incident handling agency for the U.S. civilian government, 130,000 government sites totaling 1,000,000 computer hosts were subjected to attacks in 1998 [7].

In 1999 hackers seized control of the British military communication satellite and they demanded a ransom, although British officials denied the attack ever existed [4].

In 1999 the U.S. Air Force Intelligence Agency computers were attacked by hackers believed to have originated from Russia [6].

There is a reported average of 60 to 80 percent attacks a day on U.S. Defense Department computers [8].

As all these examples demonstrate, the danger is real; the ability to unleash harm and terrorize thousands of people, thus causing widespread panic, is possessed by many. The arena to play the game is global, and there is no one who can claim the monopoly of sourcing such attacks. In the United States and probably in other countries, most attacks originating from outside the country are directed, for the moment, to military and commercial infrastructures for obvious reasons. Although most reporting of attacks seem to come from government and public infrastructures, there is a similar rate of attempts and probably success in the private sector. However, private industry is yet to become a partner with the public sector in reporting. We have already discussed the reasons why this is the case in Chapter 2.

The universality of cyber attacks creates new dimensions to cyberspace security and in fact it makes it very difficult in every aspect to predict the source of the next big one, monitor, let alone identify trouble spots, track and apprehend hackers, and put a price on the problem that is increasingly becoming a nightmare to computer systems administrators, the network community, and users in general.

Our focus in this chapter is on the price of these attacks on society. We are going to strive to put the price on the problem. However, before we do, let us try to understand the forces behind the attacks that make them thrive, the challenges in tracking the attackers and finally the price we are paying in the process.

Forces Behind Cyberspace Attacks

In the recent months, it almost looked like there was a big one every few days — a big computer network attack, that is. E-attacks are becoming not only more frequent, but also more designer-tailored, more bold, and they are taking on more systems than ever before. In fact if we look at the chronology of computer attacks, there is a progressive pattern in the number of targeted systems and severity of these attacks. Early attacks were far less dangerous and they were targeted on a few selected systems. Through the years, this pattern has been morphing, attacks becoming more daring, broader, and more indiscriminate. The latest ones including the "Love Bug," "Killer Resume," and recent DDoS, for example, have been far more devastating and indiscriminate than anything we have seen before.

The rising pattern has been confirmed in every computer crime and computer attack survey. In particular three surveys are worth noting. The CERT survey cited in Figure 2.10 (Chapter 2) shows a steady increase in the number of computer attack incidents reported to CERT from 1998 through

1999. The number of viruses also were reported to increase from 171 types in 1995 to 419 in 1999 [14]. However, this is only what has been reported to CERT; it is a small fraction of what is out there. In fact there are widely differing margins in the numbers of both reported and estimated virus types in circulation today. While the reported numbers are small, the estimated ones are quite high, some reporting as many as 53,000 virus types so far and counting [13].

In their latest 1999 most comprehensive report yet, the Computer Security Institute (CSI), in conjunction with the FBI, has reported sharp increases in all categories of e-attacks. As we pointed out in Chapter 2, while it is gratifying that the reporting of cyberspace crimes is on the rise, as indicated in these two reports, the fact is that what is reported is still a far tiny fraction of the true picture. In fact, according to reported figures, only one successful attack in 20 is ever detected by the victim and that only one of the 20 detected gets reported [6]. These figures mirror those reported by the Department of Defense, as we reported in Chapter 2. What kind of environment and fertile ground creates and keeps feeding this ever increasing phenomena? There are several reasons that we can attribute to this rather strange growth of cyber crimes.

One of these reasons is *the rapid technology growth*. This unprecedented growth in both computer and telecommunication industries has enabled access to the Internet to balloon into millions. Portable laptops and palms have made not only Internet access easier because people can now logon the Internet anytime, anywhere. But this easy access has also made the hiding places plentiful. Laptops, palms, cellular, and satellite phones have all made those "unwired" places on earth like the backyard of any urban house. From Alaska's snowcaps to the Sahara Desert to the Amazon and Congo forests, cyber access is as good as in London, New York, or Tokyo, and the arena of possible cyber attacks is growing.

Another reason is *easy availability of hacker tools*. There are an estimated 30,000 hacker-oriented sites on the Internet advertising and giving away free hacker tools and hacking tips [1]. As the Manila-generated "Love Bug" has demonstrated, hacking prowess is no longer a question of affluence and intelligence but of time and patience. With time, one can go through a good number of hacker sites, picking tips and tools, and come out with a ready payload to create mayhem in cyberspace.

Anonymity is a third reason. Those times when computer access was only available in busy well-lit public and private areas are gone. Now as computers become smaller and people with those small Internet-able gizmos become more mobile, hacker tracing, tracking, and apprehending have become even more difficult than ever before. Now they can hide in smaller places, spend a lot of time and produce deadlier viruses with very little attention drawn.

Cyber crime has also grown as a result of *cut-and-paste in programming technology.* This has removed the most important impediment that prevented many would-be hackers from trying the trade. Historically, before anybody could develop a virus, one had to write a code for it. The code had to be written in a computer programming language, compiled, and made ready to go. This means, of course, that the hacker had to know or learn a programming language! Learning a programming language is known to be not a one-day job. It takes long hours of studying and practicing. Well, today this is no longer the case. We're in an age of *cut-and-paste programming.* The pieces and technical know-how are readily available from hacker sites. One only needs to have a motive and the time.

Communications speed is another factor to consider. With the latest developments in bandwidth, high volumes of data can be moved in the shortest time possible. This means that intruders can download the payload, usually developed by cut-and-paste offline, very quickly log off and possibly leave before detection is possible.

The *high degree of internetworking* also supports cyber crime. There is a computer network in almost every country on earth. Nearly all these networks are connected on the Internet. In many countries Internet access is readily available to high percentages of the population. In the United States, for example, almost 50 percent of the population have access to the Internet [17]. On a global scale, studies show that currently up to 40 percent of developed countries and 4 percent of all developing countries on the average have access to the Internet and the numbers are growing daily [12]. As time passes, more and more will join the Internet bandwagon, creating the largest electronic human community in the history of humanity. The size of this cybercommunity alone is likely to create many temptations.

Finally, we must realize that crime is encouraged by our *increasing dependency on computers.* The ever increasing access to cyberspace, together with increasing capacity to store huge quantities of data, increasing bandwidth in communication networks to move huge quantities of data, increased computing power of computers, and computer plummeting prices have all created an environment of human dependency on computers. This, in turn, is creating numerous problems and fertile ground for hackers.

Challenges in Tracking Cyber Vandals

All the reasons we have given in the previous section are making it extremely difficult for law enforcement agencies and other interested parties like computer equipment manufacturers and software producers to track down and apprehend cybercriminals. In addition to these structural and technological bonanzas outlined above that give fertile ground to cyber-crime, there are also serious logistic challenges that prevent a successful cyber-criminal from being tracked down and apprehended. Let us consider some of those challenges.

As the computer networks sprawl grows around the globe, improve-ments in computer network technology and communication protocols are made, and as millions jump on the Internet bandwagon, the volume of traffic on the Internet will keep on growing always ahead of the technology. This makes it extremely difficult for law enforcement agencies to do their work. The higher the volume of traffic the harder it gets to filter and find cyber criminals. It is like looking for a needle in a hay stack or looking for a penny from the bottom of an ocean.

The recent distributed denial of service (DDoS) attacks have demon-strated how difficult it is to trace and track down a well-planned cyber attack. When the attackers are clever enough to mask their legitimate sources in lay-ers of multiple hoops that use innocent computers in networks, the task of tracking them becomes even more complicated. Because we explained in detail how this can be achieved in Chapter 2, we will not do so again here. However, with several layers of hoops, DDoS and other penetration attacks can go undetected.

There is a serious lack of a good hacker profile that can be used by law enforcement and other interested parties to track down would-be hackers before they create mayhem. The true profile of a computer hacker has been changing along with the technology. In fact the Manila-generated "Love Bug" demonstrated beyond doubt how this profile is constantly changing. This incident and others like it discredited the widely held computer hacker profile of a well-to-do, soccer-playing, suburban, private schooled, first-world teen. The incident showed that a teenager in an underdeveloped nation, given a computer and access to the Internet, can create as much may-hem in cyberspace as his or her counterpart in industrialized, highly com-puterized societies. This lack of a good computer hacker profile has made it extremely difficult to track down cyber criminals.

The mosaic of global jurisdictions is also making it difficult for secu-rity agencies to make cross-border tracking of cyber criminals. The Inter-net as a geographically-boundaryless infrastructure has demonstrated for the first time how difficult it is to enforce national laws on a boundaryless community. Traditionally, there were mechanisms to deal with cross-border criminals. There is Interpol, a loose arrangement between national police forces to share information and sometimes apprehend a criminal outside a country's borders. Beside Interpol, there are bilateral and multinational agreements and conventions that establish frameworks through which "international" criminals are apprehended. In cyberspace, this is not the case. However, there are now new voices advocating for a form of *cyberpol*. But even with cyberpol, there will still be a need for changing judicial and law enforcement mechanisms to speed up the process of cross-border tracking and apprehension.

There is a lack of history and of will to report cyber crimes. This is a problem in all countries. We have already discussed the reasons that still hinder cyber crime reporting.

Because of the persistent lag between technology and the legal processes that include most of the current wiretaps, cross-state and cross-border laws, effective tracing, tracking and apprehension of cyber criminals is a long way off. And as time passes and technology improves, as it is bound to, the situation will become more complicated and we may even lose the fight.

Costs of Cyberspace Attacks

As computer prices plummet, computers and Internet devices become smaller, and computer ownership and Internet access sky-rocket, cost estimating the cost of e-attacks becomes increasingly a very difficult thing to do. For one thing, each type of e-attack (seen in Chapter 3) has its own effects on the resources of cyberspace, and the damage each causes depends on the time, place, and topography used.

Then, too, it is very difficult to quantify the actual true number of attacks. Only a tiny fraction, of what everyone believes is a huge number of incidents, is detected and even a far smaller number of that is reported. In fact, as we reported in the previous section, only one in 20 of all system intrusions is detected and of those detected only one in 20 is reported [6].

Because of these small numbers reported, there has been no conclusive study to establish a valid figure that can at least give us an idea of what it is that we're dealing with. The only few known studies have been regional and sector based. For example there have been studies in education, on defense, and in a selected number of industries and public government departments.

According to Terry Guiditis, of Global Integrity, 90 percent of all computer attacks both reported and unreported is done by insiders [8]. Insider attacks are rarely reported even if they are detected. As we reported in Chapter 2, companies are reluctant to report any type of cyber attacks, especially insider ones, for fear of diluting integrity and eroding investor confidence in the company.

Another problem in estimating the numbers stems from a lack of cooperation between emergency and computer crime reporting centers worldwide. There are over 100 such centers worldwide but they do not cooperate because most are commercially competing with each other [8].

It is difficult, too, to estimate costs when faced with so many unpredictable types of attacks and viruses. Attackers can pick and choose when and where to attack. Also the types of and topography used in attacks cannot be predicted. Hence, it is extremely difficult for system security chiefs to prepare for attacks and thus reduce the costs of each attack that might occur.

Virus mutations are another issue in the rising costs of cyber attacks. The recent Code Red virus is an example of a mutating virus. The original virus started mutating after about 12 hours of release. It put enormous strain on systems administrators to search and destroy all the various strains of the virus and the exercise was like looking for a needle in a hay stack.

Another problem is the lack of trained system administrators and security chiefs in the latest network forensics technology who can quickly scan, spot, and remove or prevent any pending or reported attack and quickly detect system intrusions. Without such personnel, it takes longer to respond to and clear the system from an attack, so the effectiveness of the response is reduced. Also failure to detect intrusion always results in huge losses to the organization.

A final problem is primitive monitoring technology. The computer industry as a whole, and the network community in particular, have not achieved the degree of sophistication that would monitor a computer system continuously for full proof detection and prevention of system penetration. The industry is always on the defensive, always responding after an attack has occurred and with inadequate measures. In fact, at least for the time being, it looks like the attackers are setting the agenda for the rest of us. This kind of situation makes every attack very expensive.

Input Parameters for Cost Estimate Model

Whenever an e-attack occurs and one is interested in how to estimate the costs of such an attack, what must be considered in order to come out with a relatively good plausible measure of costs resulting from such an attack? There is not and there has not been an agreed on list of items whose costs are quantifiable from any user, hardware and software manufacturers, network administrators, or the network community as a whole. However, there are some obvious and basic parameters we can start with in building the model such as those in the list below:

(i)   actual costs in software;

(ii) actual costs in hardware;

(iii) loss in host computer time. This is computed using a known computer usage schedule and costs per item on the schedule. To compute the estimate, one takes the total system downtime multiplied by cost per scheduled item;

(iv) estimated cost in the employee work time. Again this is computed using known hourly employee payments multiplied by the number of idle time units; and

(v)   loss in productivity. This may be computed using known organizational performance and output measures.

If one has full knowledge of any or several of the items on this list and knows the type of e-attack whose cost is being estimated, one can use the model to arrive at a plausible estimate. Such estimates have been done as illustrated in the following studies.

Estimated Costs of Cyber Attacks on the Education Sector

In the first few attempts to study the costs of e-attacks on institutions of higher learning, Virginia Rezmierski of the University of Michigan in a study of 30 e-attacks found that the cost of these attacks varied widely, depending on the incident. Looking at a cross-section of those attacks she found that most attacks, of those she studied, affected only a few people. They were probably locally generated or highly focused to affect only a few people. The study found that the average attack cost less than $15,000 each to fix. However, in a few other cases that were considered as severe, whether locally generated or not, but affected more than 1000 users, the costs ran up to $100,000. The study used an array of different types of e-attacks that included hacker attacks, accidental data losses, power outages, and thefts of computer equipment. One interesting finding from the study was that the way an institution dealt with the problem had as much to do with the final cost as the nature of the attack. This one finding points to the need for a good security policy if the organization is to reduce the costs of computer attacks [7].

Computer Security Institute and FBI Study (1999)

Perhaps the most comprehensive study and estimates to date of costs of e-attacks has been done by the San Francisco–based Computer Security Institute (CSI), in coordination with the San Francisco FBI Computer Intrusion Squad. In their latest annual "Computer Crime and Security Survey" they have put a dollar amount to an array of *e-crimes*. The study was the fifth in their annual surveys of large corporations and government agencies meant to raise awareness to e-crimes in the United States. The survey involving primarily 273 large corporations and government agencies looked at 13 major categories of e-crimes. In its findings, the study revealed that for 1999 of those 273 large corporations and government agencies [8]:

(i)   Ninety percent were able to detect intrusion in their systems within a period of one year.
(ii) Seventy percent suffered financial losses.
(iii) Forty-two percent were willing or able to quantify those financial losses.

The survey findings also confirmed the following issues raised by other studies:

(i)   That most organizational e-attacks are from within. The survey found that 79 percent of those reporting indicated that attacks were from within the organization.
(ii) That most e-attacks are virus-based. The survey found that 85 percent of those reporting were affected by virus attacks.
(iii) That DDoS attacks are on the rise. The survey found that 27 percent of all e-attacks were DDoS attacks — a sharp rise from 1998 figures.
(iv) That while in the past most e-attacks were from within the organization, and many still are, there is an increasing trend in system intrusions from outside the organization. This trend is increasing because of improving computer communication technology like the Internet. The survey indicated that 25 percent of all respondents reported intrusion from outside.
(v)   That as e-commerce picks up momentum and business competitiveness increases in the global economy, the value of proprietary information is on the rise. From the survey, proprietary information was one of the categories of crimes causing the largest losses.

Overall, the 273 companies and government agencies surveyed reported an estimated annual 1999 loss of $265 million. The survey also revealed other interesting trends. In almost every category, in the three year period covered, there was a marked increase in the number of reported incidents. This trend is in line with Figure 3.1 of incidents reported to CERT.

WarRoom Research

In 1996, WarRoom Research, Inc., conducted an Information Systems Security Survey of a number of Fortune 1000 firms. Nearly half of the 205 firms that responded admitted that their computer networks had been successfully attacked. Of the 205 firms that responded to the survey:

(i) 98 firms acknowledged that their staff had detected intrusions into their systems.
(ii) 84 percent reported estimated losses and associated costs for each successful intrusion by outsiders into their computer systems was over $50,000.
(iii) 41 percent of the respondents reported losses of more than $500,000.
(iv) 36 firms reported losses of over 1 million dollars per intrusion [10].

Other Estimates

These following estimates were done by various bodies and entities but as those above, they cover a limited scope.

(i) A Study of 300 Australian companies by Deloitte Touche Tohmatsu found that over 37 percent of the companies experienced some form of security compromise in 1997, with the highest percentage of intrusions (57 percent) occurring in the banking and finance industry [16].
(ii) A 1996 survey by the American Bar Association of 1000 companies showed that 48 percent had experienced computer fraud in the last five years. Company losses were reported to have ranged from $2 to 10 million [16].
(iii) At an Ottawa, Canada, conference in early 1997, information security specialists estimated that the U.S. economy loses more than $100 billion each year through industrial espionage — a figure that has been growing at 500 percent per year since 1992 [16].
(iv) According to a Boston-based consulting firm, fear of security breeches has prompted corporations to increase their security budgets by 25 percent since 1995 [16].

Unsubstantiated Estimates

Lack of coordinated efforts to estimate the costs of e-crimes has led to a confusing situation with varying and sometimes conflicting estimates of one e-attack flying around after each attack. For example, the figures in the following examples cannot be confirmed:

(i) $1.2 billion resulting from the Canadian-generated DDoS. This figure was based on the estimates of $1 billion on stock losses, $100 million on company losses, and $100 million on system upgrades.
(ii) There is an estimated 1000 e-attacks a day on U.S. based banks.
(iii) Melissa virus cost $80 million in North America alone [5].

Social and Ethical Consequences

Although it is difficult to estimate the costs of e-attacks on physical system resources, it can be done as we have seen above. However, estimating the cost of such attacks on society is almost impossible.

For example, we are not able to put a price tag on the psychological effects, which depend on the attack motive. Attack motives that result in long psychological effects include hate and joke especially on an individual. Psychological effects may lead to individual reclusion, increasing isolation, and such trends may lead to dangerous and costly repercussions on the individual, corporations, and society as a whole.

What about the cost of moral decay? There is a moral imperative in all our actions. When human actions, whether bad or good, become so frequent, they create a level of familiarity that leads to acceptance as "normal." This type of acceptance of actions formerly viewed as immoral and bad society is moral decay. There are numerous e-attacks that can cause moral decay. In fact, because of the recent spree of DDoS, and e-mail attacks, one wonders whether people doing these acts seriously consider them as immoral and illegal any more!

We must also take into account the overall social implications. Consider the following scenario. Suppose in society X cheating becomes so rampant that it is a daily occurrence. Children born in this cheating society grow up taking cheating as "normal" since it happens always. To these children and generations after them, cheating may never ever be considered a vice. Suppose there is a neighboring society Y which considers cheating bad and immoral, and the two societies have for generations been doing commerce between them. But as cheating becomes "normal" in society X, the level of trust of the people of X by the people of Y declines. Unfortunately it won't be only the decline in trust, there will also be a corresponding decline in the business activities between the two societies. While society Y has a choice to do business with other societies that are not like X, society X loses the business with Y. This scenario illustrates a situation that is so common in today's international commerce where cheating can be like any other human vice. It also illustrates the huge hidden costs that are difficult to quantify that may cause society to suffer if it continuously condones certain vices as normal.

Then there is the cost of the loss of privacy. After the recent headline making e-attacks on CNN, eBay, E*Trade, and Amazon, and the e-mail attacks that wrenched havoc on global computers, there is a resurgence in the need for quick solutions to the problem that seems to have hit home. Many businesses are responding with patches, filters, ID tools, and a whole list of "solutions" as we will discuss in Chapter 5. Among these "solutions" are profile scanners and straight e-mail scanners like *Echlon*. Echlon is a high-tech U.S. government spying software housed in England. It is capable of scanning millions of e-mails given specific keywords. Those e-mails that are trapped by it are further processed and subsequent actions are taken as warranted. Profile scanners are a direct attack on individual privacy. This type of privacy invasion in the name of network security is a threat to all of us whose price we will never estimate and we are not ready to pay! The blanket branding of every Internet user as a potential computer attacker or a criminal until proven otherwise, by a software of course, is perhaps the greatest challenge to personal freedoms and very costly to society.

Finally, who can put a price tag on the loss of trust? Individuals, once attacked, lose trust in a person, group, company, or anything else believed to be the source of the attack or believed to be unable to stop the attack. E-attacks, together with draconian solutions cause us to lose trust in individuals, businesses, especially businesses hit either by e-attacks or trying to forcibly stop attacks. Such customer loss of trust in a business is disastrous for that business. Most importantly, it is a loss of innocence society had about computers.

As the growth of the Internet increases around the globe, computer prices plummet, Internet access becomes easier and widespread, and computer technology produces small computers and communication gadgets, the number of e-attacks are likely to increase. The current, almost weekly, reports of e-attacks on global computers is an indication of this trend. The attacks are getting bolder, more frequent, indiscriminate, widespread, and destructive. They are also becoming more difficult to detect as new programming technologies and delivery systems are developed, thus making estimating costs more complicated, difficult, specialized, and of course expensive.

Currently very few people, including system administrators and security chiefs, are able to estimate costs of many types of e-attacks. This is not likely to get better soon because of the ever increasing numbers of far better trained hackers, the pulling together of hacker resources, the creation and sharing of hacking tools, and the constantly changing attack tactics. The administrators and security personnel already overburdened with the rapidly changing security environments are not able to keep up with these fast changing security challenges. So whenever attacks occur, very few in the network community can make a good plausible estimate for any of those attacks. In fact we are not even likely to see a good estimate model soon because:

(i)   there is no one agreed on list of parameters to be used in any estimate.

(ii)   the costs, even if they are from the same type of attack, depend on incidents. The same attack may produce different losses if applied at different times on the same system.

(iii) there is a serious lack of trained technically able estimators. Very few system managers and security chiefs have the know-how to come up with good input parameters.

(iv)   many of the intrusions still go undetected; even the few detected are not properly reported.

(v)   there is no standard format for system inventory to help administrators and security experts put a price on many of the system resources.

(vi)   poor readings from ID tools can result in poor estimates. Many of the current ID tools are still giving false negatives and positives which lead to sometimes over-estimating or under-estimating the outcomes.

(vii) although systems intrusion reporting is on the rise, there is still a code of silence in many organizations that are not willing to report these intrusions for both financial and management reasons. Some organizations even undervalue the costs and underreport the extent of system intrusions for similar reasons.

(viii) depending on the sensitivity of the resources affected in an attack, especially if strategic information is involved, management may decide to under-report or undervalue the true extent of the intrusions.

Because of all these, the real cost model of e-attacks on society will be difficult to determine. We will continue to work with "magic figures pulled out of hats" for some time to come. Without mandatory reporting of e-crimes, there will never be a true picture of the costs involved. However, even mandatory reporting will never be a "silver bullet" until every sector, every business, and every individual gets involved in voluntary reporting of e-crimes.

Chapter 5

Cyber Crimes: Prevention, Detection, and System Survivability

In Chapter 2 we discussed a current list of some of the most rampant cyberspace attacks. Our discussion then was purposely focused on what those attacks were and how they affect the victim systems they attack. In Chapter 3 we categorized those attacks based on types, motives, and topography. In Chapter 4, we estimated the price of many of these attacks. In this chapter we are going to focus our discussion on the prevention and detection of e-attacks and on system survivability after an e-attack.

Preventing Cyberspace Attacks

In preventing cyberspace attacks, we want to be able to "nip the attack while it is still in the bud" so to speak. That is when such attacks are either in the planning stages and before they are downloaded, or after penetration of the system but before serious damage to the computer systems has occurred. As you would have guessed, preventing e-attacks requires advance lead information. There are several approaches to achieving this, including a good security policy, risk management, firewalls, cryptology, authentication and authorization, legislative, regulation, self-regulation, education, and a number of others.

Good Security Policy

According to RFC 2196, a security policy is a formal statement of the rules by which people who are given access to an organization's technology and information assets must abide [1]. Organization security policies are crafted to address both access and security awareness. With access the policy usually concerns itself with who is allowed to obtain information and from what source. Using various figures and percentages throughout this book, we have pointed out that most e-attacks in both private and public organizations and enterprises are from insiders. According to Keith Rhodes, director of the General Accounting Office, most successful government break-ins are from insiders [2]. These facts should underline an organization's access policy. Such policies should allow as much access as possible so that individual employees can do their assigned tasks, but full access should only be granted to those whose work calls for such access. Also the access policy, as a rule of thumb, should be communicated as fully as possible to all employees and employers. There should be no misunderstanding whatsoever.

According to Mini Subramanian, a good security policy should [3]:

(i)   identify what needs to be protected (see the list we gave in Chapter 3 of cyberspace resources that need protection);
(ii)   determine which of those items identified in (i) need to be protected from authorized access, unauthorized or unintended disclosure of information and denial of service;
(iii) determine the likelihood of the attack on those items listed in (i) above;
(iv)   implement the most effective ways that would protect those items in (i) above; and
(v)   review the policy continuously for updates if weaknesses are found.

Kaeo [4] suggests that a policy:

(i)   must be capable of being implemented technically;
(ii)   must be capable of being implemented organizationally;
(iii) must be enforceable with security tools where appropriate and with sanctions where prevention is not technically feasible;
(iv)   must clearly define the areas of responsibility for users, administrators, and management; and
(v)   must be flexible and adaptable to changing environments.

Risk Management

Risk Management is a technique to determine an organization's security measures. It involves identifying critical organization's assets, placing values on those assets, and determining the likelihood of security breaches on those assets. Risk management also involves measures to determine the level of risk acceptable to organization. In short, according to Kaeo [4], risk management involves the following steps:

(i)   Identify network assets.
(ii) Value those assets.
(iii) Determine the likelihood of threats and vulnerability of the organization. Such determination is done based on data compromise, resource availability, and loss of data integrity.
(iv) Evaluate acceptable risks for the organization.

Firewalls

A firewall is a combination of hardware and software to police network traffic that enters and leaves a network thus isolating an organization's internal network from usually a large network like the Internet. In fact, a firewall is a computer with two network cards as interfaces — that is, an ordinary router, as we discussed in Chapter 1.

According to both Smith [5] and Stalling [6], firewalls commonly use the following form of control techniques to police network traffic inflow and outflow:

(i)   Direction control: This is to determine the source and direction of service requests as they pass through the firewall.
(ii) User control: This controls local user access to a service within the firewall perimeter walls. By using authentication services like IPSec, this control can be extended to external traffic entering the firewall perimeter.
(iii) Service control: This control helps the firewall decide whether the type of Internet service is inbound or outbound. Based on this, the firewall decided on the services necessary. Such services may range from filtering traffic using IP addresses or TCP/UDP port numbers to provide an appropriate proxy software for the service.
(iv) Behavior control: This determines how particular services at the firewall are used. The firewall chooses from an array of services available to it.

Firewalls are commonly used in organizational networks to exclude unwanted and undesirable network traffic entering their organization's systems. Depending on the organization's firewall policy, the firewall may completely disallow some traffic, all the traffic, or may perform some verification on some or all of the traffic. There are two commonly used organization firewall policies:

(i)   Deny Everything: A deny-everything-not-specifically-allowed policy sets the firewall to deny all services and then add back those services allowed.
(ii) Allow Everything: In this allow-everything-not-specifically-denied policy, a firewall is set to allow everything and then deny the services considered unacceptable.

Each one of these policies enable well-configured firewalls to stop a large number of attacks. For example, by restricting and or limiting access to host systems and services, firewalls can stop many TCP-based, denial-of-service attacks by analyzing each individual TCP packet going into the network and can stop many penetration attacks by disallowing many protocols used by an attacker. In particular firewalls are needed to [7]:

(i)   prevent intruders from entering and interfacing with the operations of the organizations' network system;
(ii)   prevent intruders from deleting, or modifying information either stored or in motion within the organization's network system; and
(iii) prevent intruders from acquiring proprietary information.

There are two types of firewalls: packet filtering and application proxy. In addition, there are variations in these two types commonly called gateway or bastion.

Packet Filter Firewalls

A packet filter firewall is a multilevel firewall, in fact a router, that compares and filters all incoming and sometimes outgoing network traffic passing through it. It matches all packets against a stored set of rules. If a packet matches a rule, then the packet is accepted, if not it is rejected, or logged for further investigations. Further investigations may include deciding on further screening of the datagram, in which case the firewall directs the datagram to the screening device. After further screening, the datagram may be let through or dropped. Many filter firewalls use protocol specific filtering criteria at the data link, network, and transport layers. At each layer, the firewall compares information in each datagram like source and destination addresses, type of service requested, and the type of data delivered. A decision to deny, accept, or defer a datagram is based on one or a combination of the following conditions [7]:

- source address,
- destination address,
- TCP or UTP source and destination port,
- ICMP message type,
- payload data type, and
- connection initialization and datagrams using TCP ACK bit.

A packet filter firewall is itself divided into two configurations. One is *a straight packet filtering firewall*, which allows full-duplex communication. This two-way communication is made possible by following specific rules for communicating traffic in each direction. Each datagram is examined for the specific criteria given above and if conformity to direction-specific rules is established, the firewall lets the datagram through.

The second configuration is the *stateful inspection packet filtering firewall*, also a full-duplex filtering firewall; however, it filters using a more complex set of criteria that involves restrictions that are more than those used by a straight packet filtering firewall. These complex restrictions form a set of one-way rules for the stateful inspection filtering firewall.

Figure 5.1 on page 110 shows a packet filtering firewall in which all network traffic from source address xxx.xx.1.4 using destination port y, where y is some of the well known port numbers and x is an integer, is dropped or put in a trash. Table 5.1 on page 110 shows some of the most used application port numbers.

Application Proxy Firewalls

These types of firewalls provide higher levels of filtering than packet filter firewalls by examining individual packet data streams. An application proxy can be a small application or a part of a big application that runs on the firewall. Because there is no direct connection between the two elements communicating across the filter, unlike in the case of the packet filter firewalls, for each application generated by a communicating element, the firewall generates a proxy. The proxy inspects and forwards each application-generated traffic. Because each application proxy filters traffic based on application, it is able to log and control all incoming and outgoing traffic,

External Network   Secure Firewall   Internal Network

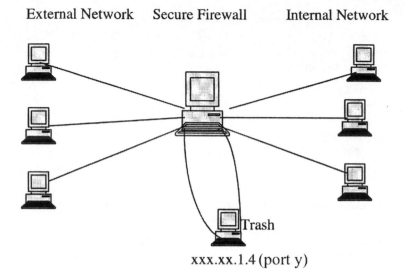

xxx.xx.1.4 (port y)

Figure 5.1 Packet Filtering Firewall

Application	Port #
Telnet	21
FTP	20, 21
WWW	80
SMTP (Email)	25

Table 5.1 Most Used Application Port Numbers

and to offer a higher degree of security and flexibility in accepting additional security functions like user level authentication, end-to-end encryption, intelligent logging, information hiding, and access restrictions based on service types. Proxy filters are shown in Figure 5.2.

Internal networks like LANs usually have multiple application proxy firewalls that may include telnet, WWW, FTP, and SMTP (e-mail). Although application proxy firewalls are great as high level filtering devices, they are more expensive to install because they may require installing a proxy firewall for each application an organization has and that can be expensive in acquiring, installing, and maintenance.

External Network   Proxy Firewall   Internal Network

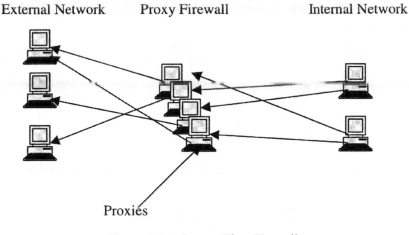

Proxies

Figure 5.2 A Proxy Filter Firewall

According to Stein [21], proxy firewalls are themselves divided into two types:

(i)   Application-level proxy firewall with the specific application proto-
      cols. For example, there is an application-level proxy for HTTP, one
      for FTP, one for e-mail, and so on. The rules of filtering they apply
      are specific to the application network packet.

(ii) Circuit-level proxy firewalls with low-level general propose protocols
      that treat all network packets as many black boxes to be forwarded
      across the filter or a bastion or not. They only filter on the basis of
      packet header information. Because of this, they are faster than their
      cousins the application-level proxies.

A combination of the filter and proxy firewalls is a gateway commonly
called a *bastion* gateway to give it a medieval castle flavor. In a firewall, packets originating from the local network and those from outside the network
can only reach their destinations by going through the filter router and then
through the proxy by station. The gateway or bastion is shown on page 112
in Figure 5.3.

Each application gateway combines a general purpose router to act as
a traffic filter and an application-specific server through which all applications data must pass.

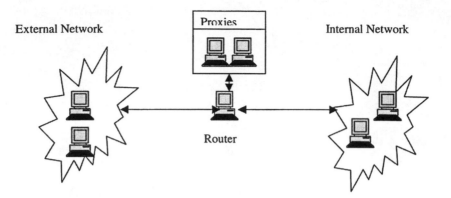

External Network

Internal Network

Proxies

Router

Figure 5.3 Application Gateway/Bastion Firewall

Cryptology

When there is no trust in the media of two communicating elements, there is always a need to "hide" the message before transmitting it through the untrusted medium. The concept of "hiding" messages is as old as humanity itself. The story has it that Julius Caeser used to "hide" his messages whenever he sent messages to his generals in battles and acquaintances. A method of "hiding" or disguising messages is called a *cryptosystem*. A cryptosystem is a collection of algorithms. Messages are disguised using these algorithms. Each algorithm has a key used to decrypt the message encrypted using that algorithm. *Cryptography* is the art of creating and using cryptosystems. The word cryptography comes from Greek meaning "secret writing." But cryptography is one side of the coin of dealing with disguised messages, the other side being that of analyzing and making sense of a disguised message. *Cryptoanalysis* is the art of breaking cryptosystems. *Cryptology*, therefore, is the study of both cryptography and cryptoanalysis. Cryptographic systems have four basic parts:

(i)   Plaintext: This is the original message before anything is done to it. It is still in either the human readable form or in a format the sender of the message created it in.

(ii) Ciphertext: This is the form the plaintext takes after it has been encrypted using a cryptographic algorithm. It is an intelligible form.

(iii) Cryptographic algorithm: This is the mathematical operations that convert the plaintext into the ciphertext.

(iv) Key: This is the tool used to turn the ciphertext into a plaintext.

There are two kinds of cryptosystems: *symmetric* and *asymmetric*.

Symmetric Encryption

In symmetric cryptosystems, usually called conventional encryption, only one key, the secret key, is used to both encrypt and decrypt a message. Figure 5.4 shows the essential elements of a symmetric or conventional encryption.

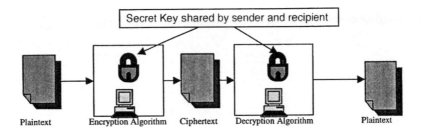

Figure 5.4 Symmetric/Conventional Encryption

Table 5.2 below lists the most common symmetric algorithms today.

Number	Algorithm	Standard	Notes
1	**DES** (Data Encryption Standard)	yes	Standardized by National Institute of Standards and Technology (NIST). Operates on 64-bit blocks, but uses 56-bit.
2	**Triple DES** (Desx, Gdes,Rdes)	No	Variant of Des-decreases risks with brute-force guessing longer keys. Uses effective 112 bit keys.
3	**RC2, RC4, RC5**	No	Proprietary algorithms by RSA Data Security, Inc. 40-bit keys. Most used by Web browsers.
4	**IDEA** (International Data Encryption Algorithm)	No	Very popular in Europe. Used in email encryption software and PGP.
5	**Blowfish**	No	Uses variable length keys of up to 448 bits. It is becoming popular.
6	**Cast-128**	No	Has variable key size of 40-128 bits. It is becoming popular. It is used in PGP.

Table 5.2 Most Used Symmetric Algorithms

For symmetric encryption to work, the two parties must find a sharable and trusted scheme to share their secret key. The strength of all those algorithms above, rests with the *key distribution* technique, a way to deliver the key to both parties. Several techniques are used including the *Key Distribution Centers* (KDC). In the KDC, each participant shares a master key with the KDC. Each participant requests for a session key from the KDC and uses the master key to decrypt the session key from the KDC.

Asymmetric Encryption

In asymmetric cryptosystems two keys are used. To encrypt a message, a public key is used and to decrypt the message a private key is used. Figure 5.5 shows the basic elements in asymmetric encryption.

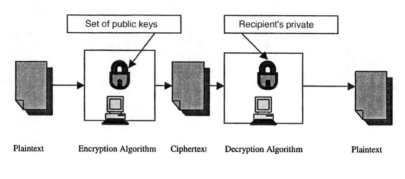

Set of public keys   Recipient's private

| Plaintext | Encryption Algorithm | Ciphertext | Decryption Algorithm | Plaintext |

Figure 5.5 Asymmetric Encryption

The public key is made available to the public and the private key is kept private. The sender encrypts the message using the recipient's public key. The recipient decrypts the ciphertext using his or her private key.

While there are many algorithms for the conventional or symmetric encryption, there are only a few asymmetric algorithms like those listed in Table 5.3 below.

Number	Algorithm	Standard	Notes
1	RSA (Ronald Rivest, Adi Shamir, Leonard Adelman)	Yes	It uses a variable key from 512 to 1,024 bits.
2	El Gamal (Taher El Gamal)	No	Uses variable key length from 512 to 1,024.

Table 5.3 Common Used Asymmetric Algorithms

Authentication and Authorization

The scheme as depicted in Figure 5.5 offers confidentiality of the message from the sender to the recipient, but does not provide the authenticity needed. It is like somebody sending an unsigned message to you. Although it can arrive safely to you, you still need to authenticate the source of the message. *Authentication* is the process of verifying the identity of a person or source of information. *Authorization* on the other hand is the process that follows authentication to grant access rights based on an identity established from authentication. The process of authentication is not an exact process because it is not based on one specific mechanism. Depending on the problem presented, different authentication mechanisms can be used to establish the needed authentication. According to RFC 1704, there are a number of different classes of authentication, ranging from no authentication to very strong authentication [8].

Using no authentication system at all is the simplest and easiest although not the best way to secure a system. For any meaningful security using no authentication, the system must be non-networked at best and a stand-alone computer or computing device in a secure location. The location may be a private place or a public facility. In a networked environment, however, user and information authentication checks are needed. These may come in many forms including user password, a physical or electronic item possessed by the user, or it may be a unique user biological feature like voice and fingerprints.

Although the primary objective of authentication is to identify users and hosts to each other, the widespread use of computer networks and the globalization of the Internet have led to the need for stronger authentication in many network services to prevent malicious users from gaining access to any information flowing over these networks. While many authentication mechanisms are simple passwords, electronic items possessed by the user, or unique user biological features, there are mechanisms that use cryptographic techniques and establish a trusted shared secret key that can be used for further exchanges during the session.

The following four authentication mechanisms are widely used:

(i) Symmetric Cryptography — which, as we saw earlier, uses the same key for both encryption and decryption.

(ii) Asymmetric Cryptography — which, unlike the symmetric cryptography, uses different keys for encryption and decryption. The technique greatly simplifies the key distribution problem.

(iii) Cryptographic Checksums — which provide data integrity and authentication but not non-repudiation.

(iv) Digital Signatures — cryptographic mechanisms that are the electronic equivalent of a written signature to authenticate a piece of data as to the identity of the sender.

Digital signatures are reversals of the public key encryption/decryption as shown in Figure 5.6 below. The session keys are shared and are obtained from the KDC as in symmetric encryption. Asymmetric cryptosystems work best when there is a trusted third party, to validate public keys. The third parties, commonly known as *Certifying Authorities* (CAs), keep all public keys of all communicating parties. During communication with any party, the sender requests for a digital certificate of the recipient, signed by the CA. From the certificate, the sender verifies the recipient's identity, and also gets the recipient's public key which he or she uses to encrypt the message before sending it to the recipient.

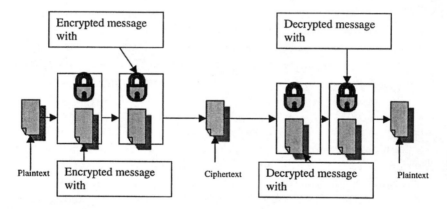

Figure 5.6 Digital Signatures

Legislation

As the Internet web grows, Internet activities increase, and e-commerce booms, the citizenry of every nation representing special interests such as environmental protection, media-carried violence, pornography, gambling, free speech, intellectual property rights, privacy, censorship, and security are grouping to put enormous pressures on their national legislatures and other law making bodies to enact laws that would curb Internet activities in ways that those groups feel best serve their interests.

Already this has started happening in countries like the United States, United Kingdom, Germany, France, China, Singapore, and the list grows every passing day. In all these countries, laws, some good, many repressive, are being enacted to put limits on the activities on the Internet. The recent upsurge of illegal Internet activities like the much publicized distributed denial of service and the headline-making e-mail attacks have fueled calls from around the world for legislative actions to be taken to stop such activities. Yet it is not likely that such actions will, at best, stop and at the least arrest the escalating rate of illegal activities in cyberspace. The patchwork of legislation will not in any meaningful way put a stop on these malicious activities in the near future. If anything, such activities are likely to continue unabated unless and until long-term plans are in place. Such efforts and plans should include first and foremost ethical education.

Regulation

As the debate between the freedom of speech advocates and protection of children crusaders heats up, governments around the world are being forced to revisit, amend, and legislate new policies, charters, and acts. As we will see in detail in the next section, this has been one of the most popular and, to politicians, the most visible means of Internet control. Legislative efforts are backed by judicial and law enforcement machinery. In the United States a number of acts are in place and are enforceable. In the last few years, many outdated acts have been re-visited and updated.

Besides purely legislative processes which are more public, there are also private initiatives that work either in conjunction with public judicial systems and law enforcement agencies or work through workplace forces. Examples abound of large companies, especially high technology companies like software, telecommunications, and Internet providers, coming together to lobby their national legislatures to enact laws to protect their interests. Such companies are also forming consortiums of some form or partnerships to create and implement private control techniques.

Self-Regulation

There several reasons why self-regulation as a means of Internet control is appealing to a good cross-section of people around the globe. One reason, supported mostly by the free-speech advocates, is to send a clear signal to governments around the world, that the World Wide Web is willing to self-regulate, rather than have the heavy hand of government legislation decide what is or is not acceptable to them.

Second there is realization that although legislation and enforcement can go a long way in helping to curb cyber crimes, they are not going to perform the magic bullet that will eventually eradicate cyber crimes. It should be taken as one of a combination of measures that must be carried out together. Probably one of the most effective prevention techniques is to give users enough autonomy to regulate themselves, each taking on the responsibility to the degree and level of control and regulation that best suits his or her needs and environment. This self-regulated cyberspace control can be done through two approaches: hardware and software.

Hardware-Based Self-Regulation

Hardware security controls and cyberspace regulation set by individual users are varied and involve controlling access to hardware resources like memory and files, authentication routines for file access, password protection, and the use of firewalls. Hardware controls are focused in six areas:

(i)   Prevention — intended to restrict access to information on the system resources like disks on network hosts and network servers using technologies that permit only authorized people to the designated areas. Such technologies include, for example, firewalls.
(ii) Protection — meant to routinely identify, evaluate, and update system security requirements to make them suitable, comprehensive, and effective.
(iii) Detection — involves deploying an early warning monitoring system for early discovery of security breaches both planned and in progress.
(iv) Limitation — intended to cut the losses suffered in cases of failed security.
(v)   Reaction — analyze all possible security lapses and plan relevant remedial efforts for a better security system based on observed failures.
(vi) Recovery — recover what has been lost as quickly and efficiently as possible and update contingent recovery plans.

Software-Based Self-Regulation

The software approach is less threatening and, therefore, more user friendly and closer to the user. This means that it can either be installed by the user on the user's computer or by a network system administrator on a network server. If installed by the user, the user can set the parameters for the level of control needed. At a network level, whether using a firewall or specific software package, controls are set based on general user consensus. Software controls fall into two categories: ratings programs and filtering programs [9].

Rating programs rate Internet content using the same principal like the movie industry uses when they rate movies for violence, language, and sex content. Software rating labels enable Internet content providers to place voluntary labels on their products according to a set of criteria. However, these labels are not uniform for the whole industry; they depend on a rating company. There are many rating companies, including Cyber Patrol, Cyber Sitter, Net Nanny, and Surf Watch, all claiming to provide a simple, yet effective rating system for web sites to protect children, and free speech for everyone who publishes on the World Wide Web. These labels are then used by the filtering program on the user's computer or server. The filtering programs always examine each web document header looking for a label.

Filtering software blocks documents and websites that contain materials designated on a filter list, usually bad words and URLs. Filters are either client-based where a filter is installed on a user's computer or server-based where they are centrally located and maintained. Server-based filters offer better security because they are not easy to tamper with. Even though filtering software, both server-based and client-based, has recently become very popular, they still have serious problems and drawbacks like inaccuracies in labeling, restriction on unrated material and just mere deliberate exclusion of certain websites by an individual or individuals. Inaccuracies have many sources. Some websites are blocked because they are near a file with some adult content. For example, if some materials are in the same directory as the file with adult content, the website with the file without adult content may be blocked. Sometimes websites are blocked because they contain words deemed to be distasteful. Such words sometimes are foreign words with completely different meanings. Further, the decision of the user to either block or unblock un-rated materials can limit the user's access to useful information. Blocking software works best only if all web materials are rated. But as we all know, with hundreds of thousands of websites submitted everyday, it is impossible to rate all materials on the Internet, at least at the moment.

Mass Education (Public Awareness)

Perhaps one of the most viable tools to prevent and curb illegal cyberspace activities is mass education. However, mass education, as good as it sounds, has its problems including the length of time it takes to bear fruit. There are many people not convinced that education alone can do the job. To them there is no time. If action is to be taken, it is time to do so. The action these people advocate is to control the Internet through a series of enforceable laws and regulations. On the other side of the debate are those who favor an unregulated Internet, an Internet free for all. There have been heated debates on both sides of the issue involving those who advocate some form of control and those who see any form of control as a death blow to the Internet as we know it today. Apparently both camps are trying to get as many people on their side as possible. In the process several different tracks have been proposed for the mass education train [9].

One of these tracks is focused education, which targets groups of the population, for example children in schools, professionals, and certain religious and interest groups. For this purpose, focused education can be subdivided into formal education and occasional or continuous education.

Formal education targets the whole length of the education spectrum from kindergarten through college. The focus and contact, however, differ depending on the selected level. For example, in elementary education, while it is appropriate to educate kids about the dangers of information misuse and computer ethics in general, the content and the delivery of that content are measured for that level. In high schools where there is more maturity and more exploratory minds, the content and the delivery system get more focused and more forceful. This approach changes in colleges because here the students are more focused on their majors and the intended education should reflect this.

Occasional or continuous education is based on the idea that teaching responsible use of information in general, and computer ethics in particular, is a lifelong process. This responsibility should be and is usually passed on to the professionals. There are a variety of ways professions enforce this education to their members. For many traditional professions, this is done through introduction and enforcement of professional codes, guidelines, and canons. Other professions supplement their codes with a requirement of in-service training sessions and refresher courses. Quite a number of professions require licensing as a means of ensuring continuing education of its members.

Reporting Centers

The recent sky-rocketing rise in e-attacks has prompted authorities looking after the welfare of the general public to open up e-attack reporting centers. The purpose of these centers is to collect all relevant information on cyber attacks and make that information available to the general public. The centers also function as the first point of contact whenever one suspects or has confirmed an electronic attack. Centers also act as advice-giving centers for those who want to learn more about the measures that must be taken to prevent, detect, and recover from attacks.

In the United States, there are several federally supported and private reporting centers including the NIST Computer Security Resource Clearinghouse, the Federal Computer Incident Response Capacity, the Center for Education and Research in Information Assurance and Security, the Carnegie-Mellon Emergency Response Team, the FedCIRC center, and the National Infrastructure Protection Center [10]. These centers fall into two categories:

(i)   non–law enforcement centers to collect, index, and advise the population of all aspects of cyber attacks including prevention, detection, and survivability.
(ii) law enforcement centers to act as a national clearinghouse for computer crime, linking up directly with other national and international computer emergency response teams to monitor and assess potential threats. In addition law enforcement centers may provide training for local law enforcement officials, and in cooperation with private industry and international law enforcement agencies. These centers do not only focus on government break-ins but also on those in the private sector, and cover any crimes perpetrated over the wires, including those involving telephones [11].

Advisories

The rise in e-attacks has also prompted collaboration between private industry and government agencies to work together to warn the public of the dangers of e-attacks and steps to take to remove the vulnerabilities thereby lessening chances of being attacked. Both major software and hardware manufacturers have been very active and prompt in posting, sending, and widely distributing advisories, vulnerability patches, and anti-virus software whenever their products are hit. Cisco, a major Internet infrastructure network device manufacturer, has been calling and e-mailing its customers, mainly Internet Service Providers (ISPs), worldwide notifying them of the possibilities of e-attacks that target Cisco's products. It also informs its customers of software patches that could be used to resist or repair those attacks. It has also assisted in the dissemination of vital information to the general public through its web sites concerning those attacks and how to prevent and recover from them. On the software front Microsoft, the most affected target in the software arena, has similarly been active posting, calling, and e-mailing its customers with the vital and necessary information on how to prevent and recover from attacks targeting its products. Besides the private sector, public sector reporting centers have also been active sending advisories of impending attacks and techniques to recover from attacks.

Detecting Cyber Attacks

It has been said that a man's house is his castle. That is where the man rules over his dominion, a dominion of stuff, a dominion of all the man's earthly resources that measure his worth. It has been said that ownership has its own psychology that attaches intrinsic value to sometimes worthless stuff. So the stuff in the man's house has intrinsic value and the man must protect it. To protect the stuff, the man must constitute a 24-hour monitoring system to alert him whenever something unusual — something with a non-normal pattern, different from the usual pattern of life in and around the house, occurs. The monitoring system the man must rely on is an alarm system that must continuously capture, analyze, and inform the man on the daily patterns of life in and around the man's house.

Detection systems deployed around a computer network system work the same way as the scenario above. They must continuously capture, analyze, and report on the daily happenings in and around the network. In capturing, analyzing, and reporting, several techniques are used including: network forensics, intrusion detection, vulnerability scanning, virus detection, and other ad-hoc methods. These techniques together offer early information to the system manager, as the alarm system in the man's house offers him an early warning for a likely or pending intrusion.

Network Forensics

Network forensics is an investigative process that studies the network environment to provide information on all issues of a healthy working network. It seeks to capture several types of network information:

(i)   network traffic and the changing traffic patterns — commonly known as traffic signatures.
(ii) the trends of individual network packet traffic. For example it gathers information on an individual network packet tracing its time of entry into the network, port number through which it entered, where is it is in the network at a specific time, how long it stays in the network, and what resources it is using and in what quantities. All this information gathered from all network packets create a sort of traffic pattern. Traffic patterns tend to follow a specific pattern for a normal operating network. Large swings in these patterns and large deviations from the norm usually signal an intrusion.
(iii) the density of traffic at specific times of the day as traffic patterns are traced, their sources and entry points in the network must be noted.

Network forensics requires that programs be provided with historic traffic patterns and the programs themselves have a degree of intelligence not only to capture, trace, and note traffic pattern variations, but most important to analyze the changes in the traffic patterns, and intelligently report to the system administrators.

The greatest benefit of network forensics is that using the information provided, network administrators can target specific abnormal traffic patterns and use them to preempt intended intrusions. If network intrusions are accurately predicted and "nipped while still in their buds," the benefits are many to the network community, ranging from completely preventing an attack to shortening an attack that had already started. In either case the process is cost effective. Much of the information network forensics uses comes from port traffic, system logs, and packet information. Let us look at these here.

Port Traffic

Many network applications send and receive data on specific port numbers. Since we discussed port numbers in Chapter 1, we will only point out here that legal port numbers range from 0 to 65535. In a normal operating network environment, specific port numbers are used by designated applications. This means that if the network is not or does not offer specific applications or does not have specific resources, the port numbers of those applications and resources will never or will rarely be activated. This sounds like a good starting point for the investigative work of network forensics. In fact in many documented network forensics, it has been found that many port numbers have been illegally used to penetrate network systems. In fact the majority of illegal network entries are through an unauthorized port. Intruders always go after well-known ports or services to execute their exploits. One of the ways to monitor port traffic is to set alarm thresholds to report connection attempts to two or more ports on a computer in a given time period, say *n* minutes. The SANS Institute has an extended list of port numbers used by Trojan viruses at http://www.sans.org/network/resources/IDFA/oddports.htm.

Logs

System logs are accounting programs that keep log files of many system activities, including: logins, connect time, user processes, mail activity, and error messages. For large systems with many activities, system log files can grow quite large and need to be truncated occasionally. In network forensics, system logs can reveal a lot of information about the network traffic. For example, logs can reveal if the system is being scanned and determine which tools are being used in the scanning.

Packet Information

As packets come into the network, each packet is looked at by a network forensics program as it builds the network traffic signature. This, however, may present a big problem when there is heavy traffic coming into the network. This, together with the disk storage space, may hinder the check on packets data for irregularities. However, there are ways to go around this problem: Murcus J. Ranum suggests that instead of collecting every packet on the network, simply record the following events [12].

- a record of the source/origin, destination port, services, bytes transferred for each TCP connection occurring on the network, and
- the URL from every web request.
- From: and To: information from all SMTP sessions, and
- the login: User-IDs from telnet, FTP, and rlogin sessions.

This reduces the amount of data to be stored and the time to analyze large quantities of data generated in heavy network traffic.

Intrusion Detection (ID)

Intrusion detection (ID) is a new technology based on the fact that software used in all cyber attacks often leaves a characteristic signature. This signature is used by the detection software and the information gathered is used to determine the nature of the attack. At each different level of network investigative work, there is a different technique of network traffic information gathering, analysis, and reporting.

Intrusion detection operates on already gathered and processed network traffic data. Designers of ID tools believe that the anomalies noticed from the analysis of this data will lead to distinguishing between an intruder and a legitimate user of the network. The anomalies resulting from the ID analyses are actually large and noticeable deviations from historical patterns of usage. ID systems are supposed to identify three categories of users: legitimate users, legitimate users performing unauthorized activities, and of course intruders who have illegally acquired the required identification and authentication.

ID sensors are commonly placed outside of all an organization's firewalls.

This usually means in the outmost organization's firewall, the last fence to the outside network, usually the Internet. This location is sometimes referred to as the *Demilitarized Zone* (DMZ). Although there are some attacks that some sensors cannot see, this location is good in being the first line of defense since all possible attacks come into the organization network through this point. Another good location for ID sensors is inside each firewall. This approach gives the sensors more protection making them less vulnerable to coordinated attacks.

As more research is done in ID and linkages are established between ID and artificial intelligence, newer ID tools with embedded extended rule-bases that enable them to learn are being developed and over time they will be able to make better analyses and, therefore, decisions. The debate is not what kind of rule-base to put in the ID tools, but what type. Currently the rule bases have been those that teach the ID tools the patterns to look for in network traffic and learn those patterns. For example, if an application is not supported by the server, that application's port number should never be active. However, the new movement differs from the traditional embedded rule-bases. The focus now is actually to embed into these ID tools what Marcus Tanum calls "artificial ignorance" which embeds into the ID tools a rule base that teaches them of things not to look for [12]. People following this line of thought believe the rule base then will be simpler and the product more effective.

The scope of ID systems is also changing in another direction. For a while now it has been assumed — wrongly — by management and many in the network community that ID systems protect network systems from outside intruders. But studies have shown that the majority of system intrusions actually are from insiders. So newer ID tools are focusing on this issue. Also, since the human mind is the most complicated and unpredictable machine ever, as new ID tools are being built to counter system intrusions, new attack patterns are being developed to take this human behavior unpredictability into account. To keep abreast of all these changes, ID systems must be constantly changing.

As all these changes are taking place, the primary focus of ID systems has been on a network as a unit where they collect network packet data by watching network packet traffic and then analyzing it based on network protocol pattern "norms," "normal" network traffic signatures, and network traffic anomalies built in the rule base. But since networks are getting larger and traffic heavier, it is becoming more and more difficult for the ID system to "see" all traffic on a switched network like an Ethernet. This has led to a new approach to looking closer at the host. So in general, ID systems fall into two categories: host-based and network-based.

Host-Based Intrusion Detection

These techniques focus on the network server to monitor specific user and application traffic handled by that server. It is actually tracking log files and audits traffic in and out of this one machine. Besides tracking in and out traffic, they also check on the integrity of system files and watch the activities of all processes on the machine for abnormal process behavior. Host-based ID systems are indeed either personal firewalls or agents. Personal firewalls, sometimes called wrappers, are configured to look at all network packets, connection attempts, and login attempts including dial-ins and non-network communications.

Agents are configured to monitor accesses and changes to critical system files and changes in user privileges [13]. Whether personal firewalls or agents, host-based ID tools are good for monitoring a network system for intrusion from insiders.

Network-Based Intrusion Detection

These tools are configured to monitor the whole network traffic including traffic on the communication media and on servers. They look for three things: signatures of known attacks, anonymous behavior, and misuse patterns [14].

Signatures of known attacks usually involve one of three common types [14]:

- String — these signatures are used to monitor text strings that may indicate a possible attack.
- Port — these signatures are used to monitor for port connection attempts. The monitoring is usually done on well-known and frequently attacked ports. Most attacked ports include port 20 for TCP, port 21 for FTP, and port 23 for telnet. A full list of TCP ports that are attacked frequently was given in earlier chapters.
- Header — these signatures monitor abnormal combinations in packet headers.

Anonymous behaviors are detected when the ID tools take observed activities and compare them to the rule-based profiles for significant deviations. The profiles are commonly for individual users, groups of users, system resource usages, and a collection of others as discussed below:

- Individual profile — a collection of common activities a user is expected to do and with little deviation from the expected norm.

This may cover specific user events like the time being longer than usual usage, recent changes in user work patterns, and significant or irregular user requests.

- Group profile — covers a group of users with a common work pattern, resource requests and usage, and historic activities. It is expected that each individual user in the group follows the group activity patterns.
- Resource profile — includes the monitoring of the use patterns of the system resources like applications, accounts, storage media, protocols, communications ports, and a list of many others the system manager may wish to include. It is expected, depending on the rule-based profile, that common uses will not deviate significantly from these rules.

Other profiles include executable profiles that monitor how executable programs use the system resources. This, for example, may be used to monitor strange deviations of an executable program if it has an embedded Trojan worm or a trapdoor virus. In addition to executable profiles, there are also the following profiles: work profile which includes monitoring the ports, static profile whose job is to monitor other profiles, periodically updating them so that those profiles cannot slowly expand to sneak in intruder behavior, and a variation of the work profile called the adaptive profile which monitors work profiles automatically updating them to reflect recent upsurges in usage. And finally there is also the adoptive rule based profile which monitors historic usage patterns of all other profiles and uses them to make updates to the rule-base [15].

Misuse patterns— that is, patterns of known misuse of system resources — are also an effective focus for ID tools. These patterns, once observed, are compared to those in the rule-base that describe "bad" or "undesirable" usage of resources. To achieve this, a knowledge database and a rule engine must be developed to work together. Misuse pattern analysis is best done by expert systems, model based reasoning, or neural networks. We will not go further in explaining how each one of these works. An interested reader is referred to a well-written paper "AINT Misbehaving: A Taxonomy of Anti-Intrusion Techniques" by R. Kenneth Bauer (http://www.sans.org/newlook/resources/IDFQA/aint.htm).

Intrusion detection tools work best when used after vulnerability scans have been performed. They then stand watch. Table 5.4 below displays several current ID tools.

Name	Source
Realsecure v.3.0	ISS
Net Perver 3.1	Axent Technologies
Net Ranger v2.2	CISCO
FlightRemohe v2.2	NFR Network
Sessi-Wall-3, v4.0	Computer Associates
Kane Security Monitor	Security Dynamics

Table 5.4 Current ID Tools

ID Criteria Matrix

The increasing numbers of ID tools on the market responding to the increasing demand for e-attacks detection, the constantly changing network technology, and the changing motives and attacks styles, all make it very difficult to craft a specific matrix of all criteria that an ID tool must have. The matrix of these capabilities is constantly changing as the technology and the whole environment of network security changes. Although there have been different evaluation criteria provided by a number of organizations, including The Metre Corporation, InfoWar.com, Information Warfare Conference, and MIT, no accepted set of criteria has emerged so far. The following set of criteria from Denmac Systems is one of the more general set of criteria in use today. For a full and more detailed list the reader is referred to the paper "Network Based Intrusion Detection: A Review of Technologies" by Denmac Systems, Inc. (http://www.nfr.net/forum/publications.html).

Criterion Name
Attack Set Detection
Protection of IDS Against IP Desync
Repetitive Attack Suppression
Alerting
Logging
Reporting
Distributed Architecture
Engine Speed
Packet Reassembly
Efficiency of Filtering
Interface Usability
Appliance/OS Implication on IDS
Maturity of Product
Product Concept
Company Focus
Price

Table 5.5 Capability Matrix

(Source: Denmac Systems, Inc.
(http://www.nfr.net/forum/publications.html)

Challenges to Intrusion Detection

While ID technology has come a long way, and there is an exciting future for it as the marriage between it and artificial intelligence takes hold, it faces many challenges. Several problems still limit ID technology.

One problem is false alarms. Though the tools have come a long way, and are slowly gaining acceptance as they gain widespread use, they still produce a significant number of both false positives and negatives.

A second problem is that the technology is not yet ready to handle a large scale attack. This is because of ID's very nature: It has to literally scan every packet, every contact point, and every traffic pattern in the network. For larger networks and in a large scale attack, it is not possible that the technology can be relied on to keep working with acceptable quality and grace. Unless there is a breakthrough today, the technology in its current state cannot handle very fast and large quantities of traffic efficiently.

Probably the biggest challenge is ID's perceived and sometimes exaggerated capabilities. The technology, while good, is not a cure of all computer network ills as some have pumped it up to be. It is just like any other good security tool.

Vulnerability Scanning

System and network scanning for vulnerability is an automated process where a scanning program sends network traffic to all computers or selected computers in the network and expects to receive return traffic that will indicate whether those computers have known vulnerabilities. These vulnerabilities may include weaknesses in operating systems, application software, and protocols.

According to Steve Jackson [16], vulnerability scanning has so far gone through three generations. The first generation required either code or script, usually downloaded from the Internet or fully distributed, to be compiled and executed for specific hardware or platforms. Because they were code and scripts that were platform and hardware specific, they always needed updates to meet specifications for newer technologies.

These limitations led to the second generation which had more power and sophistication and provided more extensive and comprehensive reports. Tools were able to scan multiple platforms and hardware and to isolate checks for specific vulnerabilities. This was a great improvement. However, they were not extensive and thorough enough, and quite often they gave false positives and negatives.

The third generation was meant to reduce those false reports by incorporating a double and sometimes triple scan of the same network resources. It used data from the first scan to scan for additional and subsequent vulnerabilities. This was a great improvement because those additional scans usually revealed more datagram vulnerabilities, the so called second level vulnerabilities. Those second level vulnerabilities, if not found in time and plugged, are used effectively by hackers when data from less secure servers is used to attack more systems servers, thus creating cascade defects in the network.

System scanning for vulnerabilities in a network is a double-edged sword. It can be used effectively by both system intruders and system security chiefs to compile an electronic inventory of the network. As the scanner continuously scans the network, it quickly identifies security holes and generates reports identifying what the holes are and where they are in the network. The information contained in the electronic inventory can be used by intruders both from inside and outside to penetrate the network and by the system security team to make the necessary security plugging of identified loopholes. So to the network security team, vulnerability scanning can have a number of benefits including the following:

- It identifies weaknesses in the network, types of weaknesses, and where they are. It is up to the security team to fix the identified loopholes.
- Once network security administrators have the electronic network security inventory, they can make a quick but thorough operating

system testing of privileges and permissions, the chief source of network loopholes, testing compliance to company policies, the most likely of network security intrusions, and finally setting up a continuous monitoring system. Once these measures are taken, it may lead to less security breaches, thus increasing customer confidence.
- When there are few and less serious security breaches, the costs for maintenance is low and the worry for loss of data is diminished.

Types of Scanning Tools

There are hundreds of network security scanning tools and scripts on the market today. Each one of these tools, when used properly, will find different vulnerabilities. As network technology changes, accompanied by the changing landscape of attacks and the advances in virus generation and other attack tools, it is difficult for any one vulnerability tool or script to be useful for a large collection of system vulnerabilities. So most security experts, to be most effective, use a combination of these tools and scripts. The most commonly used tools usually have around 140 settings carefully used to change the sensitivity of the tool or targeting the tool to focus the scan. The most common scan tools and scripts are shown in Table 5.6 below [17]:

Name	Platform/Hardware/protocol	Update			Number of scans
Nessus 1.00	Linux, BSD, Solaris, Others	yes		yes	> 250
Elza 1.4.7 (beta)	Web-based, covers most web applications and protocol	yes		yes	many
Sara 3.0.1	Based on Satan	yes		yes	many
Saint 2.0.1	Based on Satan, High-tech Interface	yes		yes	many
MNS v.91 (beta)	Auditing/Logging package	yes		yes	many
Messala 1.5 (beta)	Linux, Web-based	yes		yes	many
Bass 1.0.7	Linux, BSD, Solaris, Others	yes		yes	many
Exscan 0.4	Port Scanner (specific services)	yes		yes	Many
Narrow 2000 port 10	Sript: Red-Hut, Free BSD, Open BSD, Slackware, SUSE, Windows 9X	yes		yes	>350
Ftp Check V0.32	Network ftp application	yes		yes	ftp related
Relay Check V0.3	SMTP hosts	yes		yes	SMTP related

Table 5.6 Commonly Used Vulnerability Scanning Tools

For commercial vulnerability scanners and scripts, we will give a survey of the most current tools and scripts divided into two categories: network-based and host-based. Network-based tools are meant to guard the entire network and they scan the entire network for a variety of vulnerabilities.

They scan all Internet resources including servers, routers, firewalls, and local-based facilities. Host-based scanning is based on the fact that a large percentage of network security is from within the organization, from inside employees; it, therefore, focuses on a single host that is assumed to be vulnerable. It requires an installation on the host to scan the operating system and hardware of the machine. At the operating system level, the scanner checks on missing security checks, vulnerable service configurations, poor password policies, and bad or poor passwords. Tables 5.7 and 5.8 respectively show commonly used network-based and host-based scanning tools.

Name	Manufacturer
Enterprise Security Manager	Axent Technlogies, Inc.
System Scanner	Internet Security Systems, Inc.

Table 5.7 Network-Based Commercial Tools and Scripts

Name	Manufacturer
UltraScan/NetRecon	Axent Technologies
Internet Scanner	Internet Security Systems, Inc.
HackerShield/Netective	Netect, Inc.
Nmap	Insecure
CyberCop Scanner	Network Associates, Inc.
Kane Security Analyst	Security Dynamics Technologies, Inc.

Table 5.8 Host-Based Commercial Tools and Scripts

One of the most commonly used scanners today is Nmap, a network port scanning utility for single hosts, small, and large networks. Nmap supports many scanning techniques including Vanilla TCP connect, TCP SYN (half open), TCP FIN, Xmas, or NULL, TCP FTP proxy (bounce attack), SYN/FIN, IP fragments, TCP ACK and Windows, UDP raw ICMP port unreachable, ICMP (ping-sweep), TCP Ping, Direct (non portmapper) RPC, Remote OS Identification by TCP/IP Fingerprinting, and Reverse-identity scanning [18].

When fully configured, Nmap can perform decoy scans using any selection of TCP addresses desired by its operator. Nmap can also simulate a coordinated scan to target different networks in one country or a number of countries all at the same time. It can also hide its activities in a barrage of what appears to the user or system administrator to be multi-national attacks. It can spread out its attacks to hide below a monitoring threshold set by the system administrator or the system security team. Nmap is extremely effective at identifying the types of computers running in a targeted network and the potentially vulnerable services available on every one of them.

Virus Detection

A virus detection program, commonly called anti-virus program, is a software program that monitors or examines the system including its data and program files for the presence of viruses. Once a virus has infected the system, it is of vital importance that such a virus be removed from where it is, whether in its active or dormant stage. There are a number of techniques used by anti-virus programs to detect a virus in whatever stage a virus is in. Such techniques include detecting virus signatures, file length, checksum, and symptoms.

A virus signature is a specific and unique series of bytes bearing unique virus characteristics that is used as a human fingerprint to detect a virus. The most common of these characteristics are part of the virus instructions. Every virus have its own specific characteristics. The known characteristics are used to build up defenses to future viruses. Although there are new viruses created and distributed almost everyday, the most common viruses in circulation according to reports from virus and the e-attack reporting agencies and centers, are the same old ones. So it makes sense to use the historical facts of viruses and their characteristics and create defenses to future e-attacks. Most of today's anti-virus scanners use this technique to detect viruses in systems. One weakness with signature detection is that only known viruses can be detected. This calls for frequent updates to virus scanners to build up an archive of signatures.

File length is a useful detection item because viruses work by attaching themselves to software as their surrogates. Usually when this happens, the length of the surrogate software increases. Antivirus software works by checking the length of the original file or software and always comparing that length with the length of the file or software whenever it is subsequently used. If the two lengths differ, this signals the existence of a virus. Note that this method does not reveal the type of virus in the file or data, it only detects the presence of a virus.

A checksum is a value calculated in a file to determine if data has been altered by a virus without increasing the length of the file. There are two ways a checksum is used by anti-virus checkers. One way is to compute the total number of bytes in the file and a store it somewhere. Every time the file is used, the anti-virus software recalculates the checksum and compares it with the original checksum. If the new value differs from the stored original, then the anti-virus program reports the existence of a virus. In the second approach, probably in small files, checksum is computed as a sum of all binary words in a file. This method is better used to detect those viruses that do not, in any way, increase the length of a file but simply alter its content. In transmission data, the checksum is computed for data before it is transmitted and again after transmission. If a virus was introduced between the source and destination, the checksum will reveal it. Let us illustrate this technique by an example. Suppose the file has four 16-bit words as shown below.

$$
\begin{array}{r}
0001010110011000 \\
0011010001101100 \\
0000110011110010 \\
0111110001101110 \\
\hline
\end{array}
$$

Sum — — — — — — —   →   1101001101100100
One's complement (flips)   0010110010011010

Before the transmission, the sum of all words in the file to be transmitted is computed. It results into a binary string (16 bits in our example). To compute the one's complement, individual bits are flipped. All 0s are turned into 1s and all 1s into 0s. This word is also transmitted. At the destination, the binary sum of all transmitted words is once again computed. The resulting binary string is added to the flipped string sent along with the file. The sum should always be the string of ones. In our case: 1111111111111111. If there are any zeros in the string, the virus detection software should report the presence of either an error in transmission or a virus. Checksum should be used only when it is clear that the first time a checksum was computed the file was virus free; otherwise, it will never detect a virus if there was a virus already in the file the first time the file was used.

The symptoms of a virus, if found in a file or software, indicate the presence of a virus. Virus symptoms usually depend on the type of virus. Remember that symptoms are not unique to any one virus. Several viruses may have similar symptoms. Some of the most common symptoms are those that cause the following:

- frequent or unexpected computer reboots;
- sudden size increases in data and software;

- disappearance of data files;
- difficulty saving open files;
- shortage of memory; and
- a presence of strange sounds or text.

Ad-Hoc

In this section let us discuss some of the preventive techniques of most of the e-attacks we discussed in Chapter 2. Most of the suggested solutions in this section are based on solutions in a paper "Trends in Computer Attacks" by Elias Levy (http://www.usenix.org/publications/login/1998-5/levy.html).

Application Service Providers (ASP)

Businesses that choose to install computer networks soon find that they are in for a shocking surprise: the cost of the associated equipment is only the tip of the monetary iceberg. The major cost of owning a network is the preventive and reactionary maintenance, and the people it takes to keep the network running efficiently. Application Service Providers, or ASPs, is a new industry that has arisen over the past few years to alleviate the problems associated with trying to keep up with computer networks. They take most of the network functions, including security, outside the business to a centralized location where they offer efficient and reliable computers to take over the job of storing data, providing application software, data backup, virus checks, and a host of functions that would normally have to be performed by equipment and people in a business, especially small businesses that do not have the capacity or resources to do so. Teams of network specialists in all areas of network functionalities are available around the clock.

Patching

Quite often companies release software to the public only to find out errors and loopholes through which attackers can gain access to the resources on which the software is running. On becoming aware of these errors and loopholes, companies then issue patches in order to plug those errors. Security chiefs and system administrators should look for the most up-to-date patches from software manufacturers and vendors [19].

Configuring Hosts for Security

Newly installed operating systems on their first runs enable all available networking features of the computer system giving the hackers a chance to explore system vulnerabilities. It is advisable to turn off all unneeded network services when installing a new operating system [19].

War Dialing

Intruders often bypass a site's network security schemes by configuring their computers to receive incoming computer calls. For example, an employee can steal an employer's computer resources from home by dialing into the corporate network. The technique can be used extensively to steal telephone facilities. Intruders use war dialing programs to call a large number of telephone numbers looking for those computers allowed to receive telephone calls. They then use these as backdoors into the network. Systems administrators should regularly use war dialers to discover these back doors. Both commercial and free war dialers are readily available [19].

Network Discovery Tools and Port Scanners

Network discovery tools and port scanners can draw up an inventory of all services running on each host of the network. With this information, hackers can identify all the network vulnerabilities. The security team should use the same tools to monitor, determine, and pin-point the same vulnerabilities and plug them up [19].

IP Spoofing

We introduced and defined IP spoofing as a process of introducing into an IP network packets with fake source IP addresses, thus "spoofed" packets. It is a pillar and a building block used by other network attackers. It allows the attacker to impersonate other hosts while hiding the true origin thus making tracking the source of the network attacks a very painful process. Insidious as the problem of IP Spoofing, it has no quick fix. One way to stop IP spoofing and predictable TCP sequence numbers, as discussed in Chapter 3, is to stop the attacks at the border routers acting as firewalls configured to drop any packets coming into the network with a source address belonging to a specific network or IP address. The firewall can also stop packets with known "bad" addresses like 0.0.0.0 (all zeros broadcast), 255.255.255.255 (all ones broadcast), 127.0.0.0/8 (loopback), 10.0.0.0/8 (reserved), 172.16.0.0/12 (reserved), and 192.168.0.0/16 (reserved) from coming into the network [19].

Source Routing

The source routing feature in IP protocol allows the sender of an IP packet to pre-determine the route the packet will take as it travels through the network. When implemented in the IP protocol, source routing allows attackers to route the response packets through a segment of the network to which the attackers are attached. This allows the attackers to see the responses to their spoofed packets, responses they would otherwise not have seen. Through these responses, they obtain information such as TCP sequence numbers. To protect a network against source routing attacks, security teams should disable all source routing features in the network [19].

SYN Flooding

As we discussed in Chapter 3, SYN flooding attack sends thousands of spoofed TCP connection requests to a target network server overwhelming its resources. This may seriously slow down the server or completely bring it down. Although there is no one good solution to this problem, a number of solutions are being implemented including SYN cookies, RST cookies, random early drop, increasing the backlog queue, creating new light-weight structures to be used instead of protocol control blocks, and using hashes instead of linked lists [19].

Smurfing

In Chapter 3 we discussed a smurf attack as an attack that involves spoofing a number of ICMP echo (ping) packets with the victim's address as the source address and a directed broadcast address, an address which lets one address every address on the subnet, as the recipient. By carefully selecting a large, densely populated subnet, an attacker can generate enough traffic from the subnet hosts responding to the ping packets to consume a lot of network and host resources with a few spoofed packets [19].

According to Elias Levy, a similar attack uses the UDP echo service instead of ICMP echo packets to generate traffic that is even more devastating because the target sends back ICMP unreachable messages, thus contributing to the traffic. A working solution to this type of attack is through the observation that because there are very few applications using directed broadcast addresses, it is better to disable translation of layer 3 broadcasts into layer 2 broadcasts and ECHO and Chargen services at the router. Also hosts can be configured not to respond to broadcast ping packets or to ignore ping packets altogether [19].

Predictable Initial TCP Sequence Numbers

Again in Chapter 3 we discussed this attack as an attack that creates a one-way TCP session with the target host while spoofing another host by guessing the TCP sequence number used by the other end. The attack works by breaking down the trust relationship in the network especially in services that trust IP addresses such as the r-commands and it can only be solved through patches from vendors of operating systems.

Buffer Overflows

For UNIX operating system users and security personnel, buffer overflow is currently the most common security vulnerability to hit operating systems. We have already given the causes of buffer overflow in Chapter 3. Using a buffer overflow, an intruder attempts to overflow the buffer of a remote daemon or a setuid program to inject his machine code into the program's address space and overwrite the return address of some function. When this function returns, it executes the intruder's code creating a new process as desired by the intruder [19].

Survivability

Survivability is the capability of a system to complete the computation or a process it is currently running in favorable time bounds given savior component and environmental constraints due to an attack or accident. Survivability would include the system's capacity to withstand and gracefully complete most essential services in the presence of successful intrusion, and to recover from that intrusion.

A good survivability plan should have the following measures taken [20]:

(i) Prepare to respond to an attack by establishing policies and procedures to follow before, during, and after an attack.

(ii) Handle an attack by sticking to the following steps: prepare for an appropriate response to the attack, collect and analyze all available information, communicate the necessary information to all responsible parties, updating them periodically of the progress of the attack if and when possible, immediately implement interim short-term solution(s) to contain the attack, and bring the system back to normal operation.

(iii) Develop follow up plans that include going over the collected information to learn from the attack(s) and come up with long-term and durable solution(s) that will plug all known loopholes and vulnerabilities.

All these must be dealt with by an *Incident Response Team* (IRT).

Incident Response Team

An Incident Response Team is a primary and centralized group of dedicated people charged with the responsibility of being the first contact team whenever an incidence occurs. According to Keao [4], an IRT must have the following responsibilities:

(i)   keeping up-to-date with the latest threats and incidents;
(ii) being the main point of contact for incident reporting;
(iii) notifying others whenever an incident occurs;
(iv) assessing the damage and impact of every incident;
(v)   finding out how to avoid exploitation of the same vulnerability; and
(vi) recovering from the incident.

In handling an incident, the team must carefully do the following:

(i)   Prioritize the actions based on the organization's security policy but taking into account the following order: preserving human life and people's safety; preserving most sensitive or classified data; costly data and files; preventing damage to systems; and minimizing the destruction to systems.

(ii) Assessing incident damage: This is through doing a thorough check on all the following: system log statistics, infrastructure and operating system checksum, system configuration changes, changes in classified and sensitive data, traffic logs, and password files.

(iii) Reporting the incident to relevant parties: These may include law enforcement agencies, incident reporting centers, company executives, employees, and sometimes the public.

(iv) Recovering from the incident: This involves making a post-mortem analysis of all that went on. This post-mortem report should include steps to take in case of similar incidents in the future.

In the preceding chapters, we presented many challenges to network security. These challenges are driven by a variety of things but most remarkably advances in computer technology and lack of ethical fiber among the users. In this chapter we have concentrated on discussing the efforts being done to arrest the skyrocketing increases in cyberspace security incidents and probably prevent future illegal acts.

While the discussion in the chapter has weighed heavily on the technical side, in the two sections on avoidance and containment we focused our discussion on education because we still believe that eventually education has the best chance of arresting this ever growing menace of cyber attacks. Education, as we pointed out in the chapter, is a long haul plan which does not bear results in a year or two. It is a long term investment plan that given time always brings the trophies home in the most cost effective way, in particular computer ethics education. I want to liken computer ethics education to educating one's children. It is a twenty-something investment plan that yields lifetime dividends.

But before the delivery of the goodies, it is a long stretch of small increments sometimes with no signs to show that it is really working. However, when it all comes together, it delivers and most times handsomely. Since the ethics education we are advocating in this chapter is a long-term plan, something has to be done in the meantime and fast, because at the same time that the population is getting more computer literate — and dependent — hacker resources are getting better and more readily available, and access to the Internet is getting better, more, and global.

Because of all these, there should be no waiting; quick action is needed to arrest the situation. On one side we should be ethically educating the masses and on the other using all possible means at our disposal to reach every computer literate person young and old. In this chapter we have discussed, besides education, the technical aspects of meeting challenges. Most of the solutions or suggested solutions are changing, some becoming obsolete faster than we can write them because technology as well as the tools are constantly changing. One of the challenges of network security is to keep abreast of a rapidly changing scene of both security threats and security tools.

Chapter 6

Cyberspace and Cyber Ethics
Today and Beyond

The years since the Web component of the Internet started have been a period of excitement, bewilderment, and expansion of opportunities beyond the imagination and predictions of many. Almost every country on earth and every sector of society has experienced this excitement. Worldwide, there are an estimated 44 million Internet connections and this is doubling almost every year or so [1]. The convergence of computers, telecommunication, and broadcasting services, together with the development in Internet-abled appliances are the greatest forces behind the exploding Internet that is expected to exceed the estimated 300 million Internet users in the next few years [1].

While the Internet's effects have been felt in every sphere of society, the latest surge has been felt more and seen better in the economic growth of countries. The economic boom which started a few years ago in the United States has spread worldwide and it is affecting both developed and developing economies. This "new economy" or *e-conomy* is nothing short of a revolution. This new computer revolution spearheaded by the Internet has had a profound impact on humanity comparable, if not more, to the other revolutions; the Agricultural Revolution and the Industrial Revolution. As both the Agricultural and Industrial Revolutions changed the social, cultural, and economic status of humanity in their time, the computer revolution and the Internet, in particular, are creating waves of changes in our social, cultural, and economic dimensions.

The e-conomy promises no less impact on society. The concept, though not the facts, drove stock markets at the close of the twentieth century to unprecedented highs. Although the markets have come down from the euphoric speculative atmosphere, the momentum it started is still on, leading to creations of new *dot-com* companies and businesses that could not have existed a few years back. It is estimated that e-commerce will reach between $1.8 trillion and $3.2 trillion in the coming three to four years [1]. This unprecedented growth in the e-conomy will undoubtedly create new cyberspace industries and businesses and new professions that will challenge the traditional professions.

There is no sector of our society and in our generation that has not been profoundly changed. Changes in medical sciences and the potential for more to come is mind bogging. With fast computers, for the first time, the human gene project, the *Genome project* that maps the entire human genes is in progress. Its eventual benefits are beyond our imagination. Medical science with a good understanding of the human gene map, composition, and structure is expected to find a cure for almost all human illnesses. If the predictions of its benefits come to pass, most human illnesses will soon belong on the heap of human history. In addition to the human gene map, advances in genetic engineering and cloning are leading us into a future where we'd be able to use human replacement parts, probably ordered from eBay auction site. We may even re-create ourselves. Some believe the Internet has created new freedoms for the individual and brought new opportunities to all those connected, to do whatever they want when they want.

There have been similar and sometimes even more spectacular developments in other sectors of the old society as a result of this computer and Internet revolution. In communication, the Internet is opening up artificial and natural boundaries, bringing individuals and communities together in a fashion not seen before. The true cyberspace, as envisioned by Gibson, is actually slowly taking shape offering free flow of information across the breadth of the network at very fast speeds. Along these lines, the Internet is giving voice to those that were voiceless, providing them with an interactive media that offers millions of ears and hearts to listen, support, and offer hope. With its full-duplex communication and unlike the old one-way model of communication used by radio, television, and newspapers, the Internet is generating new civic dialogue from within the communities and from outside them, not only in those traditionally known undemocratic regions, but also in the credo of democracy where new civic networks and online voting are rejuvenating the tired democratic systems.

The social and ethical implications of all these developments on society are enormous and soon may be beyond our imagination. As it expands, creating and bringing new opportunities to the rich and famous, it almost equally brings the same opportunities to the disenchanted, the poor, and the less fortunate. This is new! We have never been in a society where everyone sets their own goals, their own laws, and chooses to obey those laws at will. It resembles the chaotic old Wild West and yet it functions well. It is a functioning anarchy that is delivering opportunities by the bucketfulls! Alas! As expected, Utopia does have both sheep and wolves. New "hot" social, moral, and ethical consequences are creeping up in Utopia and are creating heated debates of how to deal with them without sacrificing the opportunities and freedoms created by cyberspace.

Cyberspace "Hot" Issues

Suppose the next outer space extraterrestrial manned NASA spaceship discovers a Utopia, a "world" with limitless opportunities, life without problems, and where people are happy 24 hours a day. There are no community laws, geographical boundaries, no identity, and everyone is free to do whatever they want with no impunity and with full anonymity. NASA astronauts back on earth report on their wonderful discovery. Since man's quest on earth is happiness and while some have had it, many are still searching for it, to them this is an opportunity worth trying. So there is a stampede on NASA.

NASA is willing to take as many "settlers" as possible. So NASA overnight becomes the getaway to "heaven" in the universe, a place of limitless happiness.

Depending on the numbers NASA can lift, very soon Utopia finds itself overwhelmed by the numbers. And as you guessed, in a short time, as the settlers' population grows, Utopia soon needs laws and law enforcement and all the ingredients that make the pie. Among the "hot" issues rising from this stampede are issues like access to Utopia (those already there would like to screen who comes in), governance, personal freedoms, security, privacy, censorship, and intellectual property rights.

The scenario above represents cyberspace here on earth. The "hot" issues Utopians have to deal with are the same issues we cyberspacians have to deal with, issues like cyberspace access and growth, Internet governance, security, privacy, censorship, free speech, and intellectual property rights.

Cyberspace Access and Growth

According to Vint Cerf at Computers, Freedom and Privacy, there are currently 44 million Internet connections and it is estimated that the world's Internet connections are likely to grow to well over 300 million by 2000/2001. This will form about 5 percent of the world's population [1]. However, it is also estimated that by 2047, the world will have a population of over 11 billion people. Of those, it is estimated that around 25 percent will be connected, that is roughly 3 billion connections [1]. Cyberspace's explosive growth is also evidenced by the exponential rise in the number of individual web pages on the World Wide Web, a component of cyberspace. Currently according to Inktomi, the company that develops scaleable Internet infrastructure software, by the end of 1999, there were over 1 billion unique web pages [2]. The web seems to be growing at a rate three times as fast as the number of connections, which means that by the year 2047 when 3 billion connections are anticipated, cyberspace contents will probably be in trillions of individual web pages. The growth in both the number of connections and web content will create a high demand for fast transmission rates and great volumes to be moved and new technologies to bring about rapid developments in Internet traffic speed to cope with the increasing graphics and audio. If all these are to hold, there must be a corresponding planned growth of the cyberspace infrastructure to accommodate the unprecedented growth in the network bandwidth, speed, and applications.

The world is slowly becoming one huge information society where individual worthiness is measured not by how much one gets but by how much information the individual has. The strength of nations will likewise be measured and based on their ability to acquire, manage, and use information. Since more and more of today's businesses, communications, and research are taking place on the Internet, access to the Internet is crucial.

Despite the significant growth of the Internet in the last five years, computer ownership and Internet access and usage have overall been very uneven and have occurred within certain limits based on income levels, demographic groups, geographic areas, and age. Each one of these indicators shows wide and probably daunting gaps and greater disparities between haves and have-nots. The Internet has created a new category of have-nots, no longer based on education and income alone but also on possession and use of information. This uneven divide has created an unequal and unfair distribution of access to information, the *digital divide*. The "digital divide" is a phrase used to describe the fact that the world is actually divided into two types of people. Those who do have the capability, capacity, and access to computers and online access and those who do not. In a broader sense, it means those with capability, capacity, and access to modern information technology, such as the telephone, television, or the Internet. The digital divide exists between those in cities and rural areas, rich and poor, the educated and the uneducated, young and old, economic classes, different parts of the world, and globally, between the more and less industrially developed nations.

Let us look at five possible information access indicators.

The first of these indicators is geography. According to the new United Nations 1999 human development report, 88 percent of the world's 143 million Internet users are in about one or two dozen wealthy countries [3]. Currently in the year 2000, the developing world has 4 percent of the connections while the developed world is 40 percent cyber connected [4]. Yet almost 90 percent of the world's population still lives in the developing world. Geographical disparities are between countries and within countries. In the United States, one of the countries with high access percentages, minorities, especially blacks and Hispanics, are less likely to have computers and even far less likely to have Internet connections. The statistics in tables and figures below tell the story. According to the National Telecommunications Information Administration's (NTIA) 1997 survey of U.S. households with a modem shown in Table 6.1 and Figure 6.1 (see page 146), if one lived in an urban area, one was more likely to own a computer and have an online access to information than somebody in a rural area.

	Rural	Urban	Central City
Northwest	46.9	45.4	44
Midwest	37.2	48	47
South	40.7	48.7	48
West	35	47.8	48.3

Table 6.1 Percentage of U.S. Computer Households with a Modem
by Region

The second indicator is income. As Table 6.2 and Figure 6.2 using data from the NTIA study above indicate, income and race greatly affect one's ability to have access to the Internet. In every income category in Table 6.2 and Figure 6.2, blacks and Hispanics were twice as less likely to have online access as whites were.

Figures from the latest Media Metrix June 2000 survey show similar U.S. household income patterns. The report shows that those households earning less that $25,000, while they form 32.1 percent, they form only 9.7

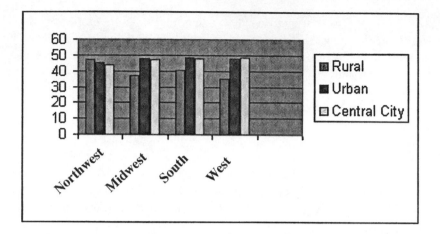

Figure 6.1 Percentage of U.S. Computer Households with a Modem
by Region

Groups	Under $15,000	15,000-34,000
White non-Hispanics	15.4	28
Black non-Hispanic	6.3	18.2
Other non-Hispanic	19.1	38.5
Hispanic	7.8	16.6

Table 6.2 U.S. Households with a Computer (1997)
by Income and Race/Origin

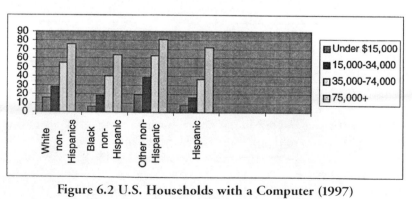

Figure 6.2 U.S. Households with a Computer (1997)
by Income and Race/Origin

percent of online users. The largest income group online according to the report earns between $40k and $60k per year, with a 27.3 percent online share, while those earning, $100k+, the highest earning bracket, have 18 percent online share [16].

Already mentioned above, race can be considered a third information access indicator. Data in Table 6.3 and Figure 6.3 of the U.S. households with a computer and a modem in the NTIA 1997 survey also confirms that blacks and Hispanics, the two main U.S. minority groups, are twice as less likely to have a computer and access to the Internet as their white counterparts.

Category	Percentage
White non–Hispanics	21.2
Black non–Hispanic	7.7
Other non–Hispanic	25.2
Hispanic	8.7

Table 6.3 U.S. Households with Online Service (1997) by Race/Origin

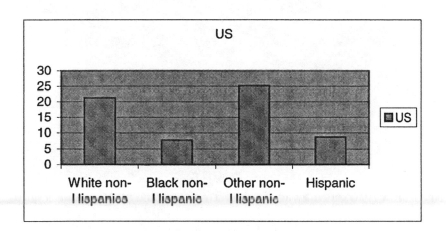

Figure 6.3 U.S. Households with Online Service (1997) by Race/Origin

Age is a fourth indicator. Older people, among all the four categories surveyed in the same NTIA 1997 report, were far less likely to have a computer and online access than the groups in their mid-twenties through their forties. Table 6.4 and corresponding Figure 6.4 both show that older people use computers and online access far less than any other age group. The latest figures from Media Metrix show similar patterns with a bell-curve-shaped usage peaking in ages 18–54 [16].

Category	Percentage
Under 25	17.1
25–34 years	22
35–44 years	24.7
45–54 years	25.8
55+ years	8.8

Table 6.4 U.S. Households with Online Service (1997) by Age

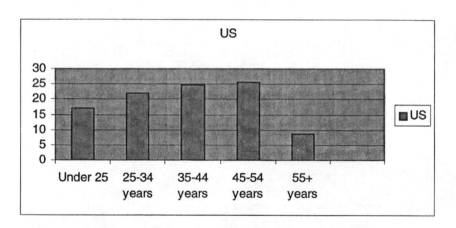

Figure 6.4 U.S. Households with Online Service (1997) by Age

The final indicator is education. Data from the NTIA 1997 survey compiled in both Table 6.5 and Figure 6.5 confirm that education has a great influence on one's access to the Internet. The higher the education level one attains the better the chances of one's Internet access.

Although these figures are based on the U.S. population only, there are strikingly similar patterns in other developed and developing countries. Much as it has been hyped as a magic development tool, the Internet may not live to deliver, at least not in its present form of global distribution unless there are better access distribution patterns based on the above five indicators.

According to Donna Hoffman of Vanderbilt University, the Internet's potential for development is there, but it will be realized only if we can get access in the hands of everyone. Otherwise, we are not likely to see revolu-

Category	Percentage
Elementary	1.8
Some HS	3.1
HS Diploma	9.6
Some College	21.9
BA or more	38.4

Table 6.5 U.S. Households with Online Service by Education

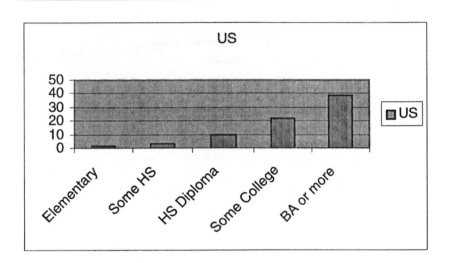

Figure 6.5 U.S. Households with Online Service by Education

tionary changes. And we will still have the schisms and chasms in society where there will be sectors of society in which people are able to partake of the wonderful riches online, and at the same time other groups are effectively excluded. If we're serious about change, we need to be thinking of getting entire countries — the developing countries and societies — online [5].

Those that are condemned to be in the *digital dark ages*, must be brought to the twenty-first century where personal worthiness and individual identity are increasingly being determined by access to information.

Cyberspace Governance

Since its inception, the governance of the Internet, and generally cyberspace, has been guided by a bottom-up, decentralized, consensus-based concept. Using this concept, the Internet made unparalleled growth and flourished beyond everyone's expectation. This concept has been carefully nurtured by many organizations and government agencies that have taken care of the Internet since its inception. And many believe it will continue to guide its future growth. The governance of the Internet and hence cyberspace since its inception has gone through various organizations and government agencies. We will focus on four periods: the ARPA era from inception through 1989, the NSF era from 1989 through 1994, the free-for-all era from 1994 through 1999, and the ICANN era after 1999.

The ARPA Era (1960–1989)

The United States, the birthplace of cyberspace, literally saw the coining of the term *cyberspace* by the science fiction novelist David Gibson. At its inception in the early 1960s, the Internet was a research project underwritten by the U.S. Department of Defense's Advanced Research Project Agency (ARPA). The research project evolved into the first computer network, called ARPANET, the baby that later grew to become the Internet. Many of the basic Internet concepts and applications like e-mail, FTP, telnet, and communication protocols began during this period. The period also saw a gradual move from defense-related research to general academic research and the development of the private industry. The period was also the start of a slow but steady growth of the Internet beyond academia and government research laboratories into homes, offices, and private commercial companies. Along with the shift from defense-related research, governance of the Internet also gradually moved away from ARPANET to the National Science Foundation (NSF).

The National Science Foundation (NSF) Era (1989–1994)

When ARPANET ceased to exist, in 1989, the National Science Foundation became the financier and overseer of the younger Internet. NSF, through its research grants programs, saw the Internet grow and mushroom into a giant. Two events of importance to the life of the Internet happened during this period. Both events contributed greatly to the explosive growth of the Internet. One was the plummeting prices of personal computers which increased personal computer ownership, and the other was the development of the World Wide Web in middle 1980s. These developments, together with the proliferation of modern technology, speeded up the growth of the Internet during the period. The NSF guided the Internet through 1994 when it quietly pulled out.

Free-for-All Era (1994–1999)

When, in 1994, the NSF Network (NSFNet), considered by many as the "jewel in the Internet Crown" was privatized, NSF relinquished its financing and babysitting duties of the Internet; it and cyberspace as a whole were considered mature enough with no more baby-feeding needed. However, at the speed the Internet was growing, it was extremely difficult to let it loose and float to find its own stability with no central body to manage it. There were a number of issues and problems many still attributable to the competing commercial networks which took over NSFNet. These commercial entities were not able to handle problems like network engineering, management, intellectual property rights, dispute resolution, and private competition. In addition to the social and structural problems, there were serious management problems resulting mainly from lack of coordination between the several private, government, and academic research agencies that were supposed to work together and govern the Internet. While there was no centralized authority to run the Internet, and cyberspace in general, between the time the National Science Foundation pulled out and 1999, there were a number of businesses, voluntary committees, and government agencies that stepped in to exert control over Internet affairs. We will divide them into the following categories: technical, business, government, and others.

A good deal of the technical work was loosely coordinated by the Internet Society (IS) consisting of the Internet Engineering Task Force (IETF), Internet Engineering Steering Group (IESG), the Internet Architecture Board (IAB), the Internet Assigned Number Authority (IANA), the Internet Research Task Force (IRTF), and the Internet Research Steering Group (IRSG).

When the National Science Foundation left the Internet scene, a number of businesses naturally stepped in to take over the tasks previously performed by the National Science Foundation. The businesses took over only those tasks that had potential for profit. There were numerous businesses mainly falling under the following categories: telecommunications like telephone companies to offer fast connection services like DSL, Internet Service Providers (ISPs), cable TV companies that offered high speed coaxial cable connections, and many hardware and software companies and Domain Name Service registrants.

Although the government, through the National Science Foundation, pulled out of the governance and physical support of the Internet and cyberspace in general, it did not actually completely relinquish its overseeing role. The government noted that the Internet was becoming a powerful communication, broadcasting, and media services channel and for a number of reasons including national security, public safety, and vital national infra-structure that used computers, the government had to keep watch over the Internet from a distance through key government agencies that included the Federal Communications Commission (FCC), the National Science Foundation (NSF), the Federal Networking Council (FNC), the National Telecommunications and Information Administration (NTIA), the Department of Commerce (DOC), and of course Congress as a legislative wing. This wing has been used a number of times to regulate the activities of the Internet including bills like the Communications Decency Act (CDA), and a few others. The government's interests have also been in keeping the vital research links open for the future directions of the Internet through its own Next Generation Internet (NGI) initiative.

At the periphery of Internet governance are other interested groups including higher education and of course a number of user groups and communities. Since the beginning of the Internet, higher education has played a critical role in its development through research partnership with industry, distance learning, and digital libraries. And as we will see shortly in the Next Generation Internet (NGI) initiative, higher education is playing its expected role in the basic research and testing. In addition to educational institutions, other organizations, mostly social, also came in responding to social issues that were of vital importance to them and the overall environment of the Internet, user organizations, and communities. Among such social organizations are the Computer Professionals for Social Responsibility (CPSR), the Electronic Frontier Foundation (EFF), American Library Association (ALA), and the American Civil Liberties Union (ALCU). Others include the WTO, EU, WIPO, OECD, UNESCO, G7/P8; also Family Research Council (FRC), Christian Coalition (CC), Electronic Privacy Information Center (EPIC), and Privacy International (PI).

The ICANN Era (1999 to Date)

After the chaos of the free-for-all era, the drifting of the Internet, the many social, political, legal, economic, and ethical problems that resulted from the period, the U.S. government through its Department of Commerce (DoC) stepped back in to help create a new governing "not-for-profit" entity. The Internet Corporation for Assigned Names and Numbers (ICANN) was formed by the private sector in response to the U.S. Department of Commerce's White Paper. In the 1998 White Paper, the U.S. government acknowledged the Internet's global reach and its potential and sought a technical management that must reflect the global diversity of its users. With this realization, it was important to make sure that the new body ensures the global Internet user community a voice in decisions that affect the Internet's technical management. These became the objectives of ICANN which was to operate for the benefits of the Internet community as a whole, in carrying out the community's activities in conformity with local, national, and international law and other relevant international conventions. It was also charged with ensuring open entry and global competition through open and transparent processes. ICANN, therefore, was to lessen the U.S. government's influence in the governance of the Internet by promoting the global public interest in the operational stability of the Internet by [6]:

(i)   coordinating the assignment of Internet technical parameters as needed to maintain universal connectivity on the Internet;
(ii) performing and overseeing functions related to the coordination of the Internet Protocol (IP) address space;
(iii) performing and overseeing functions related to the coordination of the Internet Domain Name Service (DNS), including the development of policies for determining the circumstances under which new top-level domains are added to the DNS root system; and
(iv) overseeing operations of the authoritative Internet DNS root server system.

According to the ICANN organizational chart in Figure 6.6, the organization was to be headed by a board of 19 directors to exercise the powers of ICANN. The board's presentation was to reflect the global nature of the Internet with all global Internet community interests represented according to the following formula [6]:

(i)   at least one citizen of a country located in each of the geographic regions shall serve as an At Large Director on the Board (other than the Initial Board) at all times; and
(ii) no more than one-half (½) of the total number of At Large Directors serving at any given time shall be citizens of countries located in any one geographic region. The selection of Directors by each Supporting Organization and the At Large Council shall comply with all applicable geographic diversity provisions. There are 5 ICANN geographic regions: Europe, Asia/Australia/Pacific, Latin America/Caribbean Islands, Africa, and North America. The specific countries included in each geographic region shall be determined by the Board, and this shall be reviewed by the Board from time to time to determine whether any change is appropriate, taking into account the evolution of the Internet. The 1999 geographical composition of the

ICANN Board is as follows: North America 8, Europe 7, Asia Pacific 3, Latin America 1, and Africa to be determined later. The board itself is headed by a chairman and vice-chairman who are elected annually from among the 19 board members.

The board exercises ICANN powers according to the Bylaws. The Bylaws give the board two types of voting. In certain specific issues with policies that substantially affect the operations of the Internet or third parties, including the imposition of any fees or charges, the board may act only by a majority vote of all members of the board. In all other matters the board may act by majority vote of those present at any official meeting.

Although it has a broad Internet mandate, ICANN is not supposed to act as a domain name service registry or as a registrar or Internet Protocol address registry as this would result in ICANN competing with other entities affected by the policies of the corporation. However, ICANN is mandated to protect the operational stability of the Internet in the event of financial failure of a registry or registrar or other emergency. In its decisions, the corporation is supposed to be fair in applying its standards, policies, procedures, or practices without singling out any particular party for disparate treatment unless justified by substantial and reasonable cause, such as the promotion of effective competition.

ICANN Organization Chart

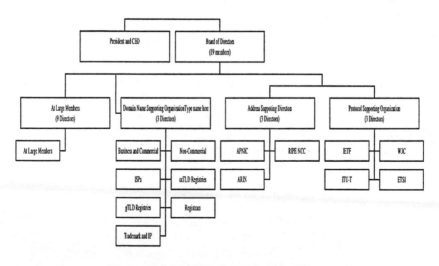

Figure 6.6 ICANN Organization Chart
(Source: http://www.icann.org/general/icann-org-chart_frame.htm)

Security

We can define security as a process or an act to prevent unauthorized access, use, alteration, and theft of property and physical damage to property. It involves three elements [7]:

- confidentiality — to prevent unauthorized disclosure of information to third parties. This is important in a number of areas including personal which may involve the disclosures of personal information like medical, financial, student academic, and criminal records.
- integrity — to prevent unauthorized modification of files and maintain the status quo. It includes system, information and personnel integrity. The alteration of information may be caused by a desire for personal gain or a need for revenge.
- availability — to prevent unauthorized withholding of information from those who need it when they need it.

Let us now discuss two types of security: physical security, which involves the prevention of access to physical facilities like computer systems, and information security, which involves prevention of access to information by encryption, authentication, and other means.

Physical Security

We consider a facility secure if it is surrounded by a physical barrier like a fence, has secure areas both inside and outside the facility, and can resist penetration by intruders. Physical security can be guaranteed if the following four mechanisms are in place [7]:

(i)   Deterrence — should be the first line of defense against intruders who may try to gain access. It works by creating an atmosphere intended to scare intruders.

(ii) Prevention — the second line of defense. Prevention mechanisms work by trying to stop intruders from gaining access.

(iii) Detection — should be the third line of defense. This mechanism assumes the intruder has succeeded or is in the process of gaining access to the system. So it tries to "see" that intruder who has gained or who is trying to gain access.

(iv) Response — an aftereffect mechanism that tries to respond to the failure of the first three mechanisms by trying to stop and prevent damage or access to a facility.

The perimeter of the facility can be secured using gadgets that prevent direct and indirect access to the facility. Such gadgets include walls, window breakage detectors, infra-red and ultrasonic detectors, animal, and human guards.

In a digital world probably most of these are not as crucial. What is needed are more electronic barriers like firewalls, encryption techniques, and passwords.

Information Security

Information security includes the integrity, confidentiality and availability of information at the servers and in transmission. Stationary information at the server can be secured using any of the physical techniques we have discussed in the preceding section. Information in transmission, however, is more difficult to secure but in general it can be secured using encryption, authentication, and audit trails at all points in the network.

Privacy

Privacy is a human value consisting of four rights. These rights are *solitude*, the right to be alone without disturbances; *anonymity*, the right to have no public personal identity; *intimacy*, the right not to be monitored; and *reserve*, the right to control one's personal information including the methods of dissemination of that information.

As humans, we assign a lot of value to these four rights. In fact these rights are part of our moral and ethical systems. With the advent of the Internet, privacy has gained even more value as information gained value. Privacy's value is embedded in its guardianship of the individual's personal identity and autonomy.

As information becomes more precious, it becomes more important for individuals to guard personal identity. Personal identity is a valuable source of information. Unfortunately, with rapid advances in technology, especially computer technology, it has become increasingly difficult to protect personal identity.

Autonomy is important because humans need to feel that they are in control of their destiny. The less personal information people have about an individual, the more autonomous that individual can be especially in decision making. However, other people will challenge one's autonomy depending on the quantity, quality, and value of information they have about that individual. People usually tend to establish relationships and associations with individuals and groups that will respect their personal autonomy, especially in decision making.

Violations of Privacy

Privacy can be violated through intrusion, misuse of information, interception of information, and information matching [7].

Intrusion, as an invasion of privacy, is a wrongful entry, seizing, or acquiring possession of property that belongs to others. As we have already seen, system intrusion is on the rise as computer networks grow.

Misuse of information is all too easy. Human beings constantly radiate information wherever they are. Every day we voluntarily give off a lot of information to whomever asks for it in order to get services. Businesses and governments collect this information from us genuinely to effectively provide services. There is nothing wrong with collecting personal information when it is going to be used for a legitimate reason, for the purpose it was intended. The information collected, however, is not always put to its intended use. It is quite often used for unauthorized purposes, hence an invasion of privacy. As commercial activities increase on the Internet, there is likely to be a stiff competition for consumer information between companies that offer services on the Internet to keep the trust of their online customers and those companies that are seeking new customers through either legally buying customer information or illegally obtaining it through eavesdropping, intrusion, and surveillance. To counter this, companies that value their customer trust and are interested in advancing their businesses are increasingly appointing new Chief Privacy Officers (CPOs) to protect not only company secrets but also their customers [14].

Interception is unauthorized access to private information by eavesdropping. Eavesdropping occurs when a third party gains unauthorized access into a private communication between two or more parties. Information can be gathered by eavesdropping in the following areas:

(i) At the source and destination of information where an individual can hide and listen in, or recording gadgets can be hidden to collect information.
(ii) Between communication channels by tapping into the communication channels and then listening in.

The threat of information matching is real. Individual behavior and characteristics can be revealed if information taken from two or more unrelated databases is put together to create an individual profile. Such profiles are compiled without authorization from the rightful person and create an invasion of privacy.

Censorship and Free Speech

The increasingly easy online access, the recent spree of hate groups, infiltration of the Internet, the availability of bomb making material, and the increasing number of pedophiles on the Internet are a few of the issues that are causing more and more people to start pointing at the Internet as a potential source of all these offensive and illegal materials that are corrupting society. Country after country are waking up to the call to do something. They are cautiously instituting Internet censorship measures in varying degrees depending on where one is.

Terrorism is not the only reason why many governments are using censorship on the Internet. Depending on where one is, the reasons given for censorship have varied from historical, social, political, and economic to cultural grounds. Other reasons to justify censorship include protection of the young and religious communities by targeting specified evils such as language use, graphic images, and video or audio.

But Internet censorship is proving to be both difficult and very expensive for those trying, and many governments and censorship bureaus are fighting a losing battle because of the exponential growth of the Internet. For governments and censorship bureaus to keep pace with this growth, they have to be continuously hiring censors, a very expensive exercise. Beside the explosive growth, Internet content is becoming highly specialized and richer in graphics which requires very expensive equipment and highly trained people to keep pace. Also the Internet's one-fits-all role of telecommunication, broadcast, and computer services is making censorship very difficult and expensive because effective censorship calls for better focus on at least one of the above, because not all these three media carry the same materials. Censors may concentrate on materials of a broadcast nature like the web pages assuming that the content they are looking for is more likely to be in this kind of medium, but may find that this is not the case, and also contents of materials change in nature and focus from time to time, from medium to medium.

Additionally cyberzens are the free-spirited individuals who care more about their freedom and are ready to fight any moves to curb that freedom by mostly changing tactics and venues. Also while the Internet's three major media, communication for e-mail, broadcast for web pages, and computer services for services like FTP, are clearly defined, it is still highly disorganized when it comes to searching for specific "content" materials which one has no prior idea about. Furthermore the Internet is presenting a situation to the courts, where the laws are chasing technology, always behind, inadequate, and with unfit modifications and clarifications of laws originally meant for old technologies like print and radio.

And finally, since the Internet is boundaryless, applying geographically defined court jurisdictions on a physical boundaryless entity is proving to be futile at best because any attempt to enforce the law in one country means enforcing the same law in a lot more than one. Case in point is the German government action to block certain sexually-oriented user groups from U.S.-based CompuServe online services in Germany a few years ago. This followed a Bavarian police investigation and charges on CompuServe to force it to block access to those objectionable areas because they violated German laws. But because CompuServe did not have the technology and software to block country by country, they ended up with a global blocking.

Many of the cyberspace problems have been brought about by the transient nature of membership in cyberspace communities. Users rarely stay in the same community with the same peers for long. These transitions are brought about by a number of reasons including changing interests, job changes, changing life styles, and a host of others. Each cyber community is a moving target community. Transients do not have allegiance and, therefore, no responsibility and accountability.

Intellectual Property Rights

Intellectual property rights form a wide scope of rights that include copyrights, patents, trademarks, trade secrets, and personal identity right.

Copyrights

Internationally copyright is a right, enforceable by law, accorded to an inventor or creator of an expression. Such expressions may include creative works like literary, dramatic, musical, pictorial, graphic, and artistic, together with audio-visual and architectural works and sound recordings. In general every original work that has a tangible form and has fixation in a medium is protectable under the copyright law.

Patents

Unlike the copyright which protects expressions, patents protect inventions or discoveries. In the United States, an invention or discovery is patentable if it meets two basic requirements [7].

The first requirement is that the invention or discovery for which the patent is sought is new and useful, or new and useful improvements of any of the following: process, manufacture (covering all products that are not machines), and machine (covering all mechanisms and mechanical products and composition of matter which includes all factory manufactured life forms).

The second requirement is that the invention or discovery must satisfy the following four conditions and all must apply:

(i)   Utility — that an invention or discovery serves a basic and minimum useful purpose to the general public or to a large percentage of the public without being a danger to the public, illegal or immoral;

(ii) Novelty — that the invention or discovery for which a patent is sought must be new, not used, known, or published somewhere before;

(iii) Non-obviousness — that the invention or discovery for which patent protection is sought must not have been obvious to anyone with ordinary skills to produce or invent in its disclosed form;

(iv) Disclosure — that there must be adequate disclosure of the product for which a patent is sought. Such a disclosure is often used by the Patent Office in its review to seek and prove or disprove the claims on the application form and also to enable the public under the contract with the government to safely and gainfully use the invention or discovery.

Trademarks

A trademark is a product or service identifying label. It is a mark that attempts to uniquely distinguish a service or a product in the minds of the consumers. The label may be any word, name, picture, or symbol. A lot of times consumers associate with the product's brand name. Since trademarks are used by consumers to choose among competing products, they are vigorously protected by their owners.

Trade Secrets

A trade secret is information that gives a company or business a competitive advantage over others in the field. This may be a formula, a design process, a device, trade figures, and more. As the above description shows, there is no one acceptable description or definition of trade secrets. The generic definition is that it is a collection of information in a given static format with strategic importance. The format may be a design expressing the information, a formula representing the collection of information, a pattern or symbol representing the information, or an insignia again representing the information. Whatever the format the collected information takes, it must have given or offered an advantage to the owner which places that owner a degree above the competition.

Personal Identity

There is a fast developing intellectual property right whose laws are being developed as the Internet technology develops. These cover such rights as the right to one's personal attributes like your social security number, name, and income which protect an individual from exploitation by others usually for personal gains. This is commonly known as personal identity. With the rapid development in computer technology, this area is becoming one of the fastest growing areas of controversy in intellectual property rights.

Intellectual property rights within each domain are protected by a body of laws and statutes. For example, copyright laws protect copyrights, patent laws protect the patent owner from infringement on his or her patent, and, although not widely used, there are laws at national and local levels that protect trademarks, trade secrets, and right of publicity. Unfortunately some of these laws are not universal; they only apply in one country, and even within a country like the United States, the same laws may not apply in all states. Because of the current jurisdiction boundaries of these laws and conventions and because of the boundaryless nature of cyberspace, the enforcement of such laws and conventions is becoming difficult. In fact a number of publishers and artists are resorting to the use of technical access controls. *Technical access controls* (TACs) are encryption techniques that create a barrier that lets an online user get some benefits of a protected material, like a web text or a music and video document, without getting all the attributes of the document a paying customer would get. For example, publishers can let a user see the document and read it on screen without printing it. Movie and music producers can let an online user watch and listen to a clip of the document without copying or downloading it. The recent Napster saga highlighted the urgency of this technology. Although this technology is promising to protect the rightful owners, the creators and inventors, it is, however, creating barriers and putting limits to many legitimate uses of the protected materials. Such restricted uses include the widely used fair use.

The New Internet

Almost every few months there are surveys and predictions giving different and sometimes conflicting figures of the expected growth of the Internet "in the next couple of years." Huge and varying as they usually are, they all point at something, that the Internet is growing fast and will keep growing for some time to come.

This explosion in the number of users will put great strains on the services provided by the Internet, and probably create infrastructure and social chaos in cyberspace. Enormous strains will be put on cyberspace resources requiring rapid and massive technical and non-technical infrastructure improvements in size, bandwidth, quality of service, and newer applications like multicasting. In addition social and ethical responsibilities need to be redefined.

Technical Demands

More technical improvements will be essential to meet demands for better and faster services with many new applications. Improved services that eliminate delays in moving information through the network will be needed. This can be achieved by improving data switching and transmission through improved network size, faster bandwidth, better quality of service, and introducing newer applications like multicasting [8].

Size

Perhaps one of the Internet growth indicators has been its size as measured by the number of users. From the original ARPANET with a limited number of a few dozen participants to the current millions of individual users, growth in size of the Internet has been spectacular. The numbers have been approximately doubling with no sign of abating. If we believe the predictions, this spectacular growth will continue well into the future. As they join the Internet bandwagon in masses, users expect "their" Internet to deliver faster and better services with a broader applications base. The anticipated explosion in e-commerce together with public data as well as government services are obvious growth dimensions in the Internet's future. Other areas of growth include directory services, routing tables and application designs to accommodate the millions of new users.

Bandwidth

New applications are putting great strains on the Internet bandwidth. Traditionally, Internet applications have used little bandwidth, except for occasional downloading of large data files. This is because the bulk of the Internet traffic, until recently, has been e-mail traffic. Electronic messages are usually in a few hundred bytes, unless they contain high graphics attachments. However, with newer applications like Napster and MP3 music that is being downloaded daily by millions of teens, end-user appetite for better high resolution databases and video content will require greater aggregate bandwidth. Along with the demand for better bandwidth, application architecture will accordingly be changed to handle broadband data streams as well as to make appropriate decisions.

Quality of Service

The phrase "Quality of Service" (QoS) consists of a wide variety of properties, including latency delay, variance jitter, and availability. Demands for improved quality of service are driven by the need for reliability, consistence, and timely delivery of control signals. To meet the high demand of QoS and accommodate changes in the computational environment of the network, Internet applications require the capability and capacity to change dynamically the levels of quality demanded by the users. As more users flock on the Internet, with varying and changing application demands, the need for continuously available services will be even greater. While the current Transport Control Protocol/Internet Protocol (TCP/IP) was designed in part to handle failures in network nodes and links, there are weaknesses in the architecture, and the newer UDP protocol does not even guarantee delivery. New user demands will call for new application architecture, new protocols, and fundamentally new software to provide services that are continuously available end-to-end, despite occasional failures of some computing elements.

Multicasting

The current Internet architecture and protocols are still running on broadcast media model with little use of multicasting. Multicasting is not currently fully supported on the present Internet because of a number of limitations in bandwidth and protocol weaknesses. Many applications that would benefit from this capability are, therefore, kept out of the Internet. For a multicasting application to use the current Internet resources, it must either use a global broadcast on a local area network or transmit multiple copies of the same information streams. This is not cost effective. Future applications will rely on multicasting to keep communication costs down and performance high.

Non-Technical Demands

Beyond these technical aspects, there will be a demand for fair and durable legislation and a mechanism to streamline a mosaic of national and regional incompatible laws that will hinder the growth of Internet commerce and communication. There will be demands for a new order for social and ethical accountability. A new mechanism will probably be needed to protect individual user privacy, the confidentiality of all data transactions, and the integrity of information on the Internet. All these and others are likely to further strain an already burdened Internet as the number of users and application requirements grow. Mindful of these needs and to allow the American industry and public to benefit from the anticipated exponential growth in computing and telecommunication, there was a need to plan for a new strategy for the Internet, a new Internet — dubbed Internet2.

Internet2

Since the resources needed to plan for the next generation Internet would overwhelm any one single institution, company, or industry, the new initiative needed to be all encompassing involving private industry, research institutions, higher learning institutions, and of course government. A number of initiatives have been set up to prepare the groundwork for the new Internet. They include the Federal Government's Information Technology for the Twenty-First Century (IT^2), the Next Generation Internet (NGI) initiatives, and the High-Performance Computing and Communication Programs (HPCC) (which we shall not discuss).

Information Technology for the Twenty-First Century (IT^2)

Information Technology for the Twenty-First Century (IT^2) is a multi-agency Federal information technology (IT) research and development (R&D) initiative commonly referred to as IT^2 initiative. It is a collaborative effort by more than 100 U.S. research universities to create and sustain a leading edge network for developing network engineering and management tools and broadband applications for advanced research and education. This initiative has three components [9]:

(i)   Long term IT research to cover research in software development for applications, human computer interfaces and information management, scaleable information infrastructure, and high end computing.

(ii) Advanced computing for science, engineering, and the nation which will include acquisition of high end systems for research, scientific, and engineering simulation software and tools, and multidisciplinary science and engineering research teams.

(iii) Research on economic, social, and workforce implications of the Information Revolution.

The Next Generation Internet Initiative (NGI)

The NGI initiative is a multi-agency Federal research and development (R&D) program that is developing advanced networking technologies, revolutionary applications that require advanced networking, and demonstrating these capabilities on testbeds that are 100 to 1000 times faster end-to-end than today's Internet. It began October 1, 1997, with the Defense Advanced Research Projects Agency (DARPA), the Department of Energy (DoE), the National Aeronautics and Space Administration (NASA), the National Institutes of Health (NIH), the National Institute of Standards and Technology (NIST), and the National Science Foundation (NSF) as participating agencies bringing in the needed capabilities and capacity.

It is managed by individual agency program managers and is coordinated by the Large Scale Networking Coordinating Group of the Interagency Working Group on Information Technology (IT) R&D of the White House National Science and Technology Council's Principals Group for IT R&D.

The NGI initiative has three goals [10]:

(i) To advance research, development, and experimentation in the next generation of networking technologies, add functionality, and improve performance.

(ii) To develop a Next Generation Internet testbed, emphasizing end-to-end performance, support networking research, and demonstrating new networking technologies. The testbed will connect at least 100 NGI sites that will include universities, Federal research institutions, and other research partners — at speeds 100 times faster than today's Internet.

(iii) To develop and demonstrate revolutionary applications that meet important national goals and missions that rely on the advances made in goals 1 and 2.

The NGI will rely on Internet2 for advanced campus-based, local-area, and select regional network infrastructure and on the private sector partners for funding. Let us now see how these goals are being implemented.

Goal 1: Experimental Research for
Advanced Network Technologies

The activities here are focusing on research, development, and testbed deployment and demonstration, of the technologies necessary to permit the effective, robust, and secure management, provisioning, and end-to-end delivery of differentiated service classes. These activities cluster into three major tasks: network growth engineering, end-to-end quality of service (QoS), and security. These technologies along with increased bandwidth will help meet the needs for dependability, differentiation of service, security, and real time demands of emerging and next generation applications such as collaboration, wide area distributed computing, and teleoperation and telecontrol. This goal is implemented by a multiagency effort led by DARPA as well as NSF, NASA, NIST, DoE, and additional contributions by non–NGI-funded agencies.

Goal 2: NGI Testbed

The testbed is currently using the following federal networks:

- NSF's very high performance Backbone Network Service (vBNS).
- NASA's Research and Education Network (NREN).
- DoD's Defense Research and Education Network (DREN).
- DoE's Energy Sciences network (ESnet).

Upon completion, it is expected to connect at least 100 sites consisting of universities, Federal research institutions, and other research partners at speeds 100 times faster end-to-end than those of today's Internet, and will connect on the order of 10 sites at speeds of between 100 Mbps to 1 Gbps that is 1000 times faster end-to-end than the current Internet. To address the inherent bottlenecks and incompatibilities in switches, routers, local area networks, and workstations, the initiative splits goal 2 into two subgoals.

The first subgoal is high performance connectivity. The NGI intends to function as a distributing laboratory delivering content at 100 times faster speeds than the current Internet performance on an end-to-end basis to at least 100 interconnected NGI participating universities, national laboratories, and Federal research sites conducting networking and applications research that require such a testbed.

The second subgoal involves NGI technologies and ultra high performance connectivity. The plan is to addresses the development of ultrahigh speed switching and transmission technologies and of end-to-end network connectivity that go beyond 1 Gbps. The outcomes of goals 1 and 2 will lay the groundwork for terabit per second (trillions of bits per second, Tbps) networks operated by appropriate network management and control and guaranteeing end-to-end quality of service.

Goal 3: Revolutionary Applications

This goal involves establishing a coordinated selection process to identify, develop, and test appropriate applications that integrate and use the advanced networking capabilities and technologies of goals 1 and 2. The selected applications are expected to be robust, realistic, complete, extensible, and adaptable to other applications. Although testbed applications are being derived from appropriate technology classes such as digital libraries, remote operation of medical instruments, environmental monitoring, crisis management, manufacturing, basic sciences, and Federal information services, applications are also being solicited from other interested research entities within academia and industry. Table 6.6 on page 168 gives a time line summary of activities as they are being implemented [11].

Global Internet Project (GIP)

The Global Internet Project (GIP) is another effort to improve the existing Internet. This international group consists of well-known leaders in the Internet revolution and senior executives of leading Internet companies in telecommunications, software, financial services, and content in North America, Asia, and Europe. GIP's objective is to foster the continued growth of the Internet worldwide.[12] For more information see http://www.gip.org.

It is amazing how fast we have become attached to the Internet given that it has been around for only a few years. The information revolution it has set in motion continues to be very important in advancing science and technology into new realms that were thought impossible just a few years back. Besides advances in science and technology, there have been parallel advances in all aspects of our lives, influencing our economic and social activities with rapid changes in commerce, incomes, education, management, information delivery, entertainment, and all other aspects of our quality of life.

If technology keeps its current pace, we are expecting many more advances in all aspects of our lives. Such advances are likely to call for better and faster information access and delivery, better applications, and more

Step #	Deliverables	First Achieved
1	1.100+ site high performance testbed providing OC-3 (155 Mbps) connections over OC-12 (644 Mbps) infrastructure	1999
2	Federal, academic, and industry partnerships conducting applications/networking research on the 100x testbed	1999
3	10+ site ultrahigh performance testbed providing OC-48 connections (2.5 Gbps)	2000
4	Networking/applications research conducted on the 1000x testbed	2001
5	Tested models for NGI protocols, management tools, QoS revisions, security, and advanced services	2000
6	100+ high value applications being tested over the high performance testbed (for example, remote, real time, collaborative NGI network control of select laboratories)	2002
7	Integrate QoS over a variety of technologies and carriers	2001
8	Terabit-per-second packet switching demonstrated	2002
9	10+ advanced applications being tested over the ultrahigh performance testbed	2002

Table 6.6 Time Line Summary of NGI Activities

bandwidth. These demands are going to put great pressure to an already strained Internet, and there will be calls for a new Internet. Plans are already underway for this new venture. As we have discussed in this chapter, if it all comes to pass and the new Internet comes to life as planned, there are going to be fundamental and unprecedented changes in our lives. We all hope the changes are for the better.

However, to achieve full potential of this anticipated Internet, it must be implemented in such a way that it will embrace all humanity, offering a full vision of its potential to all and transforming human lives in fairness.

To achieve these, the new Internet must be able to withstand and overcome many daunting challenges.

One of those challenges is equal access. While the Internet presents a vision of limitless possibilities and unbounded potential, these possibilities and potential must be brought within reach of every citizen of every nation without undue demands. These opportunities must not be brought only to those who can afford them or to those who have the capacity for them. All must be brought to the table. There are encouraging signs though indicating a gradual narrowing of this gap due mostly to the plummeting computer prices, improving user-friendliness, and ease-of-use of new systems, improving access to the cyberspace by young people at an earlier age, and higher computerization in professional, academic, and community environments.

Privacy issues also present a challenge. As information access gets easier and as more people flock to the Internet, privacy issues will heat up. The new Internet must be able to address potential information misuse. As we make strides to Internet2. A way must be found to develop privacy policies to protect individual privacy and create an environment that fosters Internet business and safeguards customer privacy [15].

Establishing a legal and regulatory framework will continue to be important. The new Internet with its expected potential will undoubtedly be a fertile ground for criminals and illegal and offensive content. It is likely to become — indeed, has already become — the main medium for hate groups, pedophilers, gamblers, money launders, and all other criminal and offensive activities. Pressure is likely to be put on governments to devise legal and regulatory mechanisms for enforcing decency and keeping the Internet healthy for all.

Another challenge will be finding a sufficient workforce. Even with the present Internet, there is already a shortage of information workers and there are predictions that if not addressed in time, this problem will escalate and perhaps compromise our national competitiveness. There must, therefore, be plans through which nations must produce a continuous and diverse supply of well-trained information personnel, particularly in engineering, computer, and information sciences.

Finally, there is the challenge of maintaining growth in the future. In order for the current Internet and the new Internet to benefit everyone, given current low participation percentages as compared to total global population, ways must be found to make it easily available to the largest population possible. In addition, Internet technology must continuously improve to keep abreast of the demands for improved access, speed, bandwidth, and applications. If all these challenges are overcome, the new cyberspace promises to be bountiful and exciting for all.

Appendix: Exercise Questions for Classroom Use

Teachers using this book in an instructional setting may find the following questions helpful in leading discussions or preparing tests on the material.

Chapter 1

1. What is a communication protocol?
2. List the major protocols for
    (i)   OSI
    (ii) TCP/IP
3. Discuss two LAN technologies that are NOT Ethernet or Token Ring.
4. Why is Ethernet technology more appealing to users than the rest of the LAN technologies?
5. What do you think are the weak points of TCP/IP?

Chapter 2

1. Why is IP spoofing a basic ingredient in many cyber attacks, especially DDoS?
2. Why have Windows NT and UNIX operating systems been a prime target of cyber attacks?
3. Suggest ways to prevent email attacks.

4. Why is it so difficult to apprehend cyber attackers outside a country?
5. Research reasons why it took the FBI a long time to apprehend the authors of the DDoS attacks on eBay, CNN and E*Trade.

Chapter 3

1. List five types of e-attacks.
2. In a short essay, discuss the differences between a denial of service attack and a penetration attack.
3. Which attack type is more dangerous to a computer system: A penetration attack or a denial of service attack?
4. What are the major differences between a boot virus and a macro virus? Which is more dangerous to a computer system?
5. List and briefly discuss five attack motives.
6. Why do hackers devote a substantial amount of time on their trade?
7. Why is civilizing the Internet a difficult task?
8. Comprehensively define "cyberspace."
9. How are viruses spread?
10. Discuss the most common security flaw.

Chapter 4

1. List and discuss the elements that make a crime an e-crime.
2. Create a list of items that you think may form a basis for a model for computing e-crime costs.
3. Discuss the challenges in tracking down cyber criminals.
4. Why is it so difficult to estimate the costs of business, national, and global e-crimes?
5. What is the best way to bring about full reporting of e-crimes, including costs?
6. Why do countries worldwide have very little information to help them combat cyber crimes?
7. Why are cyber crimes on the rise?
8. In addition to monetary costs, there are ethical and social costs of e-crimes; discuss these "hidden" costs.

Chapter 5

1. Why is a security plan so important in the security of a network?
2. Discuss the advantages and disadvantages of filtering.

3. If you were a network security chief, which of the following items would you put more emphasis on? Why?
   (i) Prevention
   (ii) Detection
   (iii) Survivability
4. How can a system security team avoid an e-attack?
5. In a short essay discuss the measures being undertaken in each of the following categories to prevent e-attacks:
   (i) Prevention
   (ii) Detection
   (iii) Survivability
6. Discuss the merits of legislating Internet policies.
7. Why is self-regulation a viable Internet control tool?

Chapter 6

1. List and discuss two cyberspace "hot" issues that need to be addressed urgently.
2. Discuss the best way to deal with the uneven distribution of cyberspace access and growth.
3. How will the goals of NGI impact the social and ethical environment of cyberspace?
4. Discuss the social and ethical implications of the New Internet (in its proposed form).
5. There is an international controversy about ICANN administrative structure. Research and discuss the merits of ICANN in the governance of the Internet.
6. There is a noticeably slow but growing narrowing of the digital divide gap. List and discuss the facts that are contributing to this.
7. Why do you think there is no gender digital divide?
8. There is a heated debate on how to deal with the big digital divide between developing and developed countries. Why do you think it is a controversial issue?
9. Discuss the ways privacy can be violated. How can such violations be stopped?
10. Why is Internet censorship difficult to stop?
11. List and discuss the rights under the umbrella of Intellectual Property Rights (IPR). How can IPR be safeguarded in cyberspace?
12. Discuss the challenges the new Internet has to overcome in order to serve all humanity fairly.

Notes

Chapter 1

1. William Stallings. *Local and Metropolitan Area Networks*. Sixth Edition, Prentice Hall, 2000.

2. Douglas E. Comar. *Computer Networks and Intranets*. Prentice Hall, 1997.

3. _____. *Internetworking with TCP/IP: Principles, Protocols, and Architecture*. Fourth Edition, Prentice Hall, 2000.

4. James F. Kurose and Keith W. Ross. *Computer Networking: A Top-Down Approach Featuring the Internet*. Addison-Wesley, 2000.

5. Mani Subramanian. *Network Management: Principles and Practice*. Addison-Wesley, 2000.

Chapter 2

1. Netscape. "'Love Bug' Computer Virus Wreaks Fresh Havoc." http://www.mynetscape.com/news/.

2. CNN. "Canadian Juvenile Charged in Connection with February 'Denial of Service' Attacks." http://cnn.com/2000/TECH/computing/04/15/hacker.arrest.01.html.

3. Merike Kaeo. Designing Network Security: A Practical Guide to Creating a Secure Network Infrastructure. Cisco Press, 1999.

4. CNN. "Mitnick Schools Feds on Hacking 101." http://cnn.com/2000/TECH/computing/03/03/mitnick.the.prof/mitnick.the.prof.html.

5. CERT/CC. "Statistics 1988-1999." Software Engineering Institute. Carnegie Mellon University. http://www.cert.org/stat/cert-stat.html.

6. ABC News. "Online and Out of Line: Why Is Cybercrime on the Rise, and Who Is Responsible?" http://www.ABCNews.com/sections/us/DailyNews/cybercrime_000117.html.

7. "Security in Cyberspace." U.S. Senate Permanent Subcommittee on Investigations, June 5, 1996. http://www.fas.org/irp/congress/1996_hr/s9606053.html.

Chapter 3

1. "Section A: The Nature and Definition of Critical Infrastructure." http://www.nipc. gov/nipcfaq.htm.
2. William Stallings. *Cryptography and Network Security: Principles and Practice.* Second Edition, Prentice Hall, 1998.
3. Peter J. Denning. *Computers Under Attack: Intruders, Worms and Viruses.* ACM Press, 1990.
4. Karen Forcht. *Computer Security Management.* Boyd & Fraser Publishing, 1994.
5. Fed Fiserberg, David Dries, Juris Hurtmanis, Don Hoocomb, M. Stuart Lynn, and Thomas Suntoro. "The Cornell Commission: On Morris and the Worm." In Peter J. Denning. *Computers Under Attack: Intruders, Worms and Viruses.* ACM Press, 1990.
6. Stepheson. "Preventive Medicine." *LAN Magazine,* November 1993.
7. Andrew Grosso. "The Economic Espionage Act: Touring the Minefields." *Communications of the ACM,* 43(8), August 2000, 15–18.
8. Don Seely. "Password Cracking: A Game of Wits." In Peter J. Denning. *Computers Under Attack: Intruders, Worms and Viruses.* ACM Press, 1990.
9. F. Grampp and R. Morris. "UNIX Operating System Security." *AT&T Bell Laboratories Tech J.,* 63, 8, Part 2 (October 1984), 1649.
10. Peter G. Neumann. "Risks of Insiders." *Communications of the ACM,* 42(12), December 1999, 160.
11. Wally Bock. "The Cost of Laptop Theft." http://www.bockinfo.com/docs/laptheft.htm.
12. Steven Levy. *Hackers: Heroes of the Computer Revolution.* Anchor Press/Doubleday, 1984.
13. Clifford Stoll. "Stalking the Wily Hacker." In Peter J. Denning. *Computers Under Attack: Intruders, Worms and Viruses.* ACM Press, 1990.
14. Calof Jonathan. "Increasing Your CIQ: The Competitive Intelligence Edge." http://www.edco.on.ca/journal/item22.htm.
15. David Noack. "The Top 10 Computer Security Flaws: An Alphabet Soup of Back Doors for Hackers." *APBNews.com,* June 2, 2000.
16. National Institute of Standards and Technology. "Computer Attacks: What They Are and How to Defend Against Them." *ITL Bulletin,* May 1999. http://www.nist.gov/itl/lab/bulletns/.
17. "SCO SNMPd Default Writeable Community String." http://www.securiteam.com/unixfocus/SCO_SNMPd_default_writeable_community_string.html.
18. ZDNet. "How Viruses Work: Some Common Viruses." http://www.zdnet.com/pcmay/pctech/content/18/03/tn1003.06.html.
19. Sophas Virus Information. "Glossary of Virus Types." http://www.sophas.com/virusinfo/articles/virustypes.html.

Chapter 4

1. John Christensen. "Bracing for Guerilla Warfare in Cyberspace." CNN Interactive, April 6, 1999.
2. Security in Cyberspace: U.S. Senate Permanent Subcommittee on Investigations. June 5, 1996.
3. "Pentagon Wave Red Over Computer Attacks." Scripps Howard & Nando News. April 7, 1998. http://www.Nando.net.
4. "Melissa Virus Writer Pleads Guilty." Sophas. http://www.sophas.com/virusinfo/articles/melissa.htm.
5. "Federal Cybersleuth Armed with First Ever Wiretap Order Nets International Hacker Charged with Illegally Entering Harvard and U.S. Military Computers." News Release. http://www.uddoj.gov/opa/pr/1996/March26/146.txt.
6. David S. Alberts. "Information Warfare and Deterrence — Appendix D: Defensive

War: Problem Formation and Solution Approach." http://www.ndu.edu/inns/books/ind/appd.htm.

7. *Chronicle of Higher Education*, July 17, 1998.

8. "Hacker Sittings and News: Computer Attacks Spreading (11/19/99)." http://www.infowav.com/hacker/99/hack-11/1999-b.shtml.

9. "The Cost of Computer Crime." Computer Security Institute. http://www.gosci.com/losses.htm.

10. CSI Press Release. http://www.gocsi.com/prelea_000321.htm.

11. CNN Headline News, June 2, 2000.

12. CNN Headline News, May 28, 2000.

13. McAfee Virus Information Center. "Virus Alerts." http://www.vil.nai.com/villib/alpha.asp.

14. Carnegie Mellon University. CERT Coordination Center. "CERT/CC Statistics 1998-1999." http://www.cert.org/stats/cert-stats.html.

15. U.S. Department of Justice. News Release March 1, 1998. "Israel Citizen Arrested in Israel for Hacking U.S. and Israel Government Computers." http://www.usdoj.gov/opa/pr/1998/march/125.htm.html.

16. "Section A: The Nature and Definition of Critical Infrastructure." http://www.nipc.gov/nipcfaq.htm.

17. "Falling Through the Net: Towards Digital Inclusion." NTIA 2000. http://www.ntia.doc.gov/ntiahome/.

Chapter 5

1. B. Fraser. "Site Security Handbook." RFC 2196, September 1997, http://www.freesoft.org/CIE/RFC/rfc-ind.html.

2. Mary Mosquera. "Most Computer Attacks Come from Organizations." TechWeb. http://www.infowar.com/hacker/99/hack_091599a_j.shtml.

3. M. Subramann. *Network Management: Principles and Practice*. Addison-Wesley, 2000.

4. Mcrike Kaeo. *Designing Network Security: A Practical Guide to Creating a Secure Network Infrastructure*. Cisco Press, 1999.

5. R. Smith. *Internet Cryptography*. Addison-Wesley, 1997.

6. William Stallings. *Cryptography and Network Security: Principles and Practice*. Second Edition. Prentice Hall, 1998.

7. J. Kurose and Keith Ross. *Computer Networking: A Top-Down Approach Featuring the Internet*. Addison-Wesley, 2000.

8. N. Haller and R. Atkinson. "Internet Authentication." RFC 1704, October 1994. http://www.freesoft.org/CIE/RFC/rfc-ind.html.

9. Joseph M. Kizza. *Civilizing the Internet: Global Concerns and Efforts Towards Regulation*. McFarland, 1998.

10. "Computer Attacks: What They Are and How to Defend Against Them." *ITL Bulletin*, May 1999.

11. Janet Kornblum. "Federal Unit to Fight Hacking" CNET NEWS.COM. http://archive.abcnews.go.com/sections/tech/CNET/cnet_hacking0227.html, http://www.nist.gov/itl/lab/bulletins/may99.html.

12. Marcus J. Tanum. "Network Forensics: Network Traffic Monitoring." http://www.nfr.net/forum/publications/monitor.html.

13. Stephen Northcutt. *Network Intrusion Detection: An Analyst's Handbook*. New Riders Publishing, 1999.

14. "Intrusion Detection: FAQ, v1. 33: What Is Host-Based Intrusion Detection?" http://www.sans.org/newlook/resources/IDFAQ/host-based.html.

15. Kenneth R. Bauer, "AINT Misbehaving: A Taxonomy of Anti-Intrusion Techniques." http://www.sans.org/newlook/resources/IDFQA/aint.htm.

16. Steve Jackson. "ESM NetRecon: Ultrascan." http://www.si.com.au/Appendix/NetRecon%20Ultrascan%20technology.html.

17. Whitehats. "Risk Assessment." http://www.whitehats.com/tools/vuln.html.

18. "Nmap — The Network Mapper." http://www.insecure.org/nmap/.

19. Elias Levy. " Trends in Computer Attacks." USENIX. http://www.usenix.org/publications/login/1998-5/levy.html.

20. Software Engineering Institute, Carnegie-Mellon University. "Responding to Intrusions." http://www.cert.org/security-improvement/modules/m06.html.

21. Lincoln Stein. *Web Security: A Step-by-Step Reference Guide*. Addison-Wesley, 1998.

Chapter 6

1. Vint Cerf. "The Internet Is for Everyone." *The Internet Society*. http://www.isoc.org/isoc/media/speeches/foreveryone.shtml.

2. "News & Events: Web Surpasses One Billion Documents." *Inktomi*. http://www.inktomi.com/news/press/billion.html.

3. James W. McConnaghery, Wendy Laden, Richard Chin, and Douglas Everette. "Falling Through the Net II: New Data on the Digital Divide." http://www.ntia.doc.gov/ntiahome/net2/falling.html.

4. "Vital Signs." CNN Headlines News, Saturday, May 28, 2000.

5. "(fwd:) Information Age Have and Have-nots." http://www.library.wustl.edu/~listmgr/devel-l/august1998/00058.html.

6. "Communication from the Commission to the Council and the European Parliament." The Commission of the European Communities (Com2000), 202. http://www.europa.eu.int/eur-lex/en/com/pdf/2000/com2000_0202en01.pdf.7.

7. Joseph M. Kizza. *Ethical and Social Issues in the Information Age*. Springer, 1999.

8. "Evolving the High Performance Computing and Communications Initiative to Support the Nation's Information Infrastructure — Executive Summary." http://www.nap.edu/readingroom/books/hpcc/exec.html.

9. "Evolving the High Performance Computing and Communications Initiative to Support the Nation's Information Infrastructure." http/www.nap.edu/readingroom/books/hpcc/contents.html.

10. "Information Technology for the Twenty-First Century: A Bold Investment in America's Future." http://www.ccic.gov/pubs/it2-ip/.

11. "High Performance and Communications Implementation Plan." National Coordination Office for Computing, Information, and Communications Interagency Working Group on Information Technology Research and Development. http://www.ccic.gov/pubs/imp99/ip99-00.pdf.

12. "New Convergence Challenges Emerge Says Group of Internet Company Executives." http://www.isoc.org/internet/issues/publicpolicy.gipo0052-.shtml.

13. Robert Fox. "News Track: Prioritizing Privacy." *Communications of the ACM*, Volume 43(9), September 2000, 9.

14. Robert Fox. "News Track: Age and Sex." *Communications of the ACM*, Volume 43(9), September 2000, 9.

15. "PITAC — Report to the President: Socioeconomic Research Priorities." http://www.ccic.gov/report/section_4.html.

16. Anne Rickert. "The Dollar Divide: Web Usage Patterns by Household Income." Media Metrix, Inc., August 2000, http://www.mediametrix.com/data/MMXI-USHHI-0600.pdf.

Bibliography

ABC News. "Online and Out of Line: Why Is Cybercrime on the Rise, and Who Is Responsible?"
http://www.ABCNews.com/sections/us/DailyNews/cybercrime_000117.html

Alberts, David S. "Information Warfare and Deterrence — Appendix D: Defensive War: Problem Formation and Solution Approach."
http://www.ndu.edu/inns/books/ind/appd.htm

Bauer, Kenneth R. "AINT Misbehaving: A Taxonomy of Anti-Intrusion Techniques."
http://www.sans.org/newlook/resources/IDFQA/aint.htm

Black, Ulysses. *Internet Security Protocols: Protecting IP Traffic*. Prentice Hall, 2000.

Bock, Wally. "The Cost of Laptop Theft."
http://www.bockinfo.com/docs/laptheft.htm

Bowyer, Kevin. *Ethics and Computing: Living Responsibly in a Computerized World*. IEEE Computer Society Press, 1996.

Bynum, Terrell (Ed.). *Computers and Ethics*. Basil Blackwell, 1985.

Calof, Jonathan. "Increasing Your CIQ: The Competitive Intelligence Edge."
http://www.edco.on.ca/journal/item22.htm

Carnegie Mellon University. CERT Coordination Center. "CERT/CC Statistics 1988-1999."
http://www.cert.org/stats/cert-stats.html

Cassel, Lillian, and Richard H. Austing. *Computer Networks and Open Systems: An Application Development Perspective*. Jones and Partlett Publishers, 2001.

Cerf, Vint. "The Internet Is for Everyone." *The Internet Society*.
http://www.isoc.org/isoc/media/speeches/foreveryone.shtml

CERT/CC. "Statistics 1988-2000." Software Engineering Institute. Carnegie-Mellon University.
http://www.cert.org/stat/cert-stat.html

Christensen, John. "Bracing for Guerilla Warfare in Cyberspace." CNN Interactive, April 6, 1999.

CNN. "Canadian Juvenile Charged in Connection with February 'Denial of Service' Attacks."
   http://cnn.com/2000/TECH/computing/04/15/hacker.arrest.01.html
___. "Mitnick Schools Feds on Hacking 101."
   http://cnn.com/2000/TECH/computing/03/03/mitnick.the.prof/mitnick.the.prof.html
Comar, Douglas E. *Internetworking with TCP/IP: Principles, Protocols, and Architecture*. Fourth Edition. Prentice Hall, 2000.
___. *Computer Networks and Intranets*. Prentice Hall, 1997.
"Communication from the Commission to the Council and the European Parliament." The Commission of the European Communities (Com2000).
   http://www.europa.eu.int/eur-lex/en/com/pdf/2000/com2000_0202en01.pdf.7
"The Cost of Computer Crime." Computer Security Institute.
   http://www.gosci.com/losses.htm
CSI Press Release.
   http://www.gocsi.com/prelea_000321.htm
Denning, Peter J. *Computers Under Attack: Intruders, Worms and Viruses*. ACM Press, 1990.
Epstein, Richard. *The Case of the Killer Robot*. John Wiley & Sons, 1997.
"Evolving the High Performance Computing and Communications Initiative to Support the Nation's Information Infrastructure."
   http://www.nap.edu/readingroom/books/hpcc/contents.html
"Evolving the High Performance Computing and Communications Initiative to Support the Nation's Information Infrastructure — Executive Summary."
   http://www.nap.edu/readingroom/books/hpcc/exec.html
Fiserberg, Fred, David Dries, Juris Hurtmanis, Don Holcomb, M. Stuart Lynn, and Thomas Suntoro. "The Cornell Commission: On Morris and the Worm." In Peter J. Denning, *Computers Under Attack: Intruders, Worms and Viruses*. ACM Press, 1990.
Forcht, Karen. *Computer Security Management*. Boyd & Fraser Publishing, 1994.
Fox, Robert. "News Track: Age and Sex." *Communications of the ACM* 43(9), September 2000, pg 9.
___. "News Track: Prioritizing Privacy." *Communications of the ACM*, 43(9), September 2000, pg 9.
Fraser, B. " Site Security Handbook." RFC 2196, September 1997.
   http://www.freesoft.org/CIE/RFC/rfc-ind.html
Grampp, F., and Morris, R. "UNIX Operating System Security." *AT&T Bell Laboratories Tech J.*, 63(8), Part 2, October 1984, pg. 1649.
Grosso, Andrew. " The Economic Espionage Act: Touring the Minefields." *Communications of the ACM*, 43(8), August 2000, pg. 15–18.
"Hacker Sittings and News: Computer Attacks Spreading (11/19/99)."
   http://www.infowav.com/hacker/99/hack-11/1999-b.shtml
Haller, N., and R. Atkinson. "Internet Authentication." RFC 1704, October 1994.
   http://www.freesoft.org/CIE/RFC/rfc-ind.html
Hester, Micah, and Paul Ford. *Computers and Ethics in the Cyberage*. Prentice Hall, 2001.
"High Performance and Communications Implementation Plan." National Coordination Office for Computing, Information, and Communications Interagency Working Group on Information Technology Research and Development.
   http://www.ccic.gov/pubs/imp99/ip99-00.pdf

"Information Age Have and Have-Nots."
  http://www.library.wustl.edu/~listmgr/devel-l/august1998/00058.html
"Information Technology for the Twenty-First Century: A Bold Investment in America's Future."
  http://www.ccic.gov/pubs/it2-ip/
"Intrusion Detection: FAQ, v1. 33: What Is Host-Based Intrusion Detection?"
  http://www.sans.org/newlook/resources/IDFAQ/host-based.html
Jackson, Steve. "ESM NetRecon: Ultrascan."
  http://www.si.com.au/Appendix/NetRecon%20Ultrascan%20technology.html
Johnson, Deborah G. *Computer Ethics*. Third Edition. Prentice Hall, 2001.
Kaeo, Merike. *Designing Network Security: A Practical Guide to Creating a Secure Network Infrastructure*. Cisco Press, 1999.
Kizza, Joseph M. *Civilizing the Internet: Global Concerns and Efforts Towards Regulation*. McFarland, 1998.
___. *Ethical and Social Issues in the Information Age*. Springer, 1999.
___. (Ed.). *Social and Ethical Effects of the Computer Revolution*. McFarland, 1996.
Kornblum, Janet. "Federal Unit to Fight Hacking." CNET NEWS.COM.
  http://archive.abcnews.go.com/sections/tech/CNET/cnet_hacking0227.html
  http://www.nist.gov/itl/lab/bulletins/may99.html
Kurose, James F., and Keith W. Ross. *Computer Networking: A Top-Down Approach Featuring the Internet*. Addison-Wesley, 2000.
Leveson, Nancy. *Safeware: System Safety and Computers*. Addison-Wesley, 1995.
Levy, Elias. "Trends in Computer Attacks." USENIX.
  http://www.usenix.org/publications/login/1998-5/levy.html
Levy, Steven. *Hackers: Heroes of the Computer Revolution*. Anchor Press/Doubleday, 1984.
McAffee Virus Information Center. "Virus Alerts."
  http://www.vil.nai.com/villib/alpha.asp
McConnaghery, James W., Wendy Laden, Richard Chin, and Douglas Everette. "Falling Through the Net II: New Data on the Digital Divide."
  http://www.ntia.doc.gov/ntiahome/net2/falling.html
"Melissa Virus Writer Pleads Guilty." Sophas.
  http://www.sophas.com/virusinfo/articles/melissa.htm
Mosquera, Mary. "Most Computer Attacks Come from Organizations." TechWeb.
  http://www.infowar.com/hacker/99/hack_091599a_j.shtml
National Institute of Standards and Technology. "Computer Attacks: What They Are and How to Defend Against Them." *ITL Bulletin*, May 1999.
  http://www.nist.gov/itl/lab/bulletns/
Netscape. "'Love Bug' Computer Virus Wreaks Fresh Havoc."
  http://www.mynetscape.com/news/
Neumann, Peter G. "Risks of Insiders." *Communications of the ACM*, 42(12) December 1999, pg. 160.
"New Convergence Challenges Emerge Says Group of Internet Company Executives."
  http://www.isoc.org/internet/issues/publicpolicy.gipo0052-.shtml
"News & Events: Web Surpasses One Billion Documents." *Inktomi*.
  http://www.inktomi.com/news/press/billion.html
"NMAP — The Network Mapper."
  http://www.insecure.org/nmap/

Noack, David. "The Top 10 Computer Security Flaws: An Alphabet Soup of Back Doors for Hackers." *APBNews.com*, June 2, 2000.

Northcutt, Stephen. *Network Intrusion Detection: An Analyst's Handbook*. New Riders Publishing, 1999.

"Pentagon Wave Red Over Computer Attacks." Scripps Howard & Nando News. April 7, 1998.
  http://www.Nando.net

"PITAC — Report to the President: Socioeconomic Research Priorities."
  http://www.ccic.gov/report/section_4.html

Proctor, Paul E. *The Practical Intrusion Detection Handbook*. Prentice Hall, 2001.

Rickert, Anne. "The Dollar Divide: Web Usage Patterns by Household Income." Media Metrix, Inc., August 2000.
  http://www.mediametrix.com/data/MMXI-USHHI-0600.pdf

"SCO SNMPd Default Writeable Community String."
  http://www.securiteam.com/unixfocus/SCO_SNMPd_default_writeable_community_string.html

"Section A: The Nature and Definition of Critical Infrastructure."
  http://www.nipc.gov/nipcfaq.htm

"Security in Cyberspace." U.S. Senate Permanent Subcommittee on Investigations, June 5, 1996.
  http://www.fas.org/irp/congress/1996_hr/s9606053.html

Seely, Don. "Password Cracking: A Game of Wits." In Peter J. Denning. *Computers Under Attack: Intruders, Worms and Viruses*. ACM Press, 1990.

Smith, R. *Internet Cryptography*. Addison-Wesley, 1997.

Software Engineering Institute, Carnegie-Mellon University. "Responding to Intrusions."
  http://www.cert.org/security-improvement/modules/m06.html

Sophas Virus Information. "Glossary of Virus Types."
  http://www.sophas.com/virusinfo/articles/virustypes.html

Stallings, W. *Cryptography and Network Security: Principles and Practice*. Second Edition. Prentice Hall, 1998.

Stallings, William. *Local and Metropolitan Area Networks*. Sixth Edition. Prentice Hall, 2000.

Stein, Lincoln. *Web Security: A Step-by-Step Reference Guide*. Addison-Wesley, 1998.

Stepheson, P. "Preventive Medicine." *LAN Magazine*, November 1993.

Stoll, Clifford. "Stalking the Wily Hacker." In Peter J. Denning, *Computers Under Attack: Intruders, Worms and Viruses*. ACM Press, 1990.

Subramanian, Mani. *Network Management: Principles and Practice*. Addison-Wesley, 2000.

Tanum, Marcus J. "Network Forensics: Network Traffic Monitoring."
  http://www.nfr.net/forum/publications/monitor.html

U.S. Department of Justice. "Israel Citizen Arrested in Israel for Hacking U.S. and Israel Government Computers." News Release March 1, 1998.
  http://www.usdoj.gov/opa/pr/1998/march/125.htm.html

"Vital Signs." CNN Headlines News. Saturday, May 28, 2000.

Whitehats. "Risk Assessment."
  http://www.whitehats.com/tools/vuln.html

ZDNet. "How Viruses Work: Some Common Viruses."
  http://www.zdnet.com/pcmay/pctech/content/18/03/tn1003.06.html

Index